Belief in Joy

PETER WILKINSON is a priest in the Archdiocese of Liverpool. He studied theology at universities in Rome and Manchester, and has been a member of the staffs of the Senior Seminaries at Upholland and Ushaw. Until his appointment as parish priest to St Clares's, Liverpool, in 1987, he had served as a member of the staff at the Upholland Northern Institute. He has been Secretary both of the Catholic Theological Association and the Episcopal Theology Commission of England and Wales. He is the author of the book: *Focus on the Sacraments*, Kevin Mayhew 1987.

Belief in Joy

The Creed
Not Dogma but Prayer

Peter Wilkinson

Kevin
Mayhew

First published in 1995 by
KEVIN MAYHEW LTD
Rattlesden
Bury St Edmunds
Suffolk IP30 0SZ

ISBN 0 86209 671 5
Catalogue No 1500029

Cover design by Veronica Ward
and Graham Johnstone

Front cover: *The Adoration of the Shepherds*
by Abraham Hondius (cira 1625/30-1695)
by courtesy of Christie's Images, London

Edited by Michael Forster
Typesetting and Page Creation by Vicky Brown
Printed and bound in Great Britain

CONTENTS

Foreword

FOREWORD

FAITH IS for freedom not for restriction. The boundaries of faith are the marking out of truth: not to enclose us in fences for control but to allow us to run in the fields of God's friendship.

The Creed is not dogma but a prayer. It is thanksgiving for blessings we have received. We are created for friendship with God; faith is the gift of that friendship; these are its basic blessings.

Friendship needs boundaries for the freedom in which to grow. The Creed gives us those boundaries: it is not for fettering but for the freedom of the spirit; the appeal is not to the head but to the whole person: heart, mind, soul and spirit.

Dogmatic statements of the Creed may appear dry, dull and carrying the dust of years. This book blows the dust away and quickens into life the low fires of faith which have always been housed in the phrases of the Fathers. The book rekindles the fires of friendship to which time-honoured words have only been offered as fuel.

All dogma, like statements of truth, are invitations to love, peace and joy: *Love* of a caring God who bothered to create and come to us; *Peace* in the possession of divine guarantees of a future rooted in God's fidelity; and *Joy* in the knowledge that all is gift and nothing has to be earned or bought.

The simplicity of the exposition hides the depth of learning which is brought to this work. There is a deceptive gentleness in the words; but they are as powerful as a breath blowing on the coals of the Creed until they glow with the Spirit they contain.

We are made for joy and to enable others and all things to enjoy the gift of life. The Creed is part of that enabling experience. It is given so that we may believe and in that belief find joy.

AELRED SMITH
Minsteracres

To the People of St Clare's

CHAPTER ONE

I BELIEVE IN GOD

CAN WE BE SURE OF GOD?[1]

We are made in the image and likeness of God and so it is natural that there should be some signs of the presence of God within human experience. In the words of the Psalmist: 'The heavens and the earth proclaim the glory of God' (cf Psalms 8:1; 19:1-6). Nevertheless, the signs are ambiguous. And so, from time to time, we are tempted to ask ourselves: 'What is the point of going on living? Am I created, known, and loved by someone who gives me a purpose and a future or is life simply a tale told by an idiot, full of sound and fury, signifying nothing?[2] Is the whole thing an awful mistake? Is there, in fact, a God, or is all talk of religion and faith in God mere fantasy?'

In Pain: where is our God?

Such questioning would seem to be justified when we reflect on the degree of pain in our world, especially the pain of so many innocent people. When a person's world has fallen apart because of tragedy of one kind or another, all manner of prayer and faith in God would seem to be utterly impossible. There is nothing left but the feeling of devastation: 'Why should this happen to me? I've tried to be a good person. I have a family who need me. I don't deserve this. Why should God make me suffer like this?' Indeed, is there anyone there to listen to such an anguished cry? In the face of so much evil and suffering which surrounds us, how can we possibly believe in a God who is all-powerful and all-loving? Either God is unable to prevent evil, in which case he is not all powerful; or he does not will to do so, in which case he is not all loving. There is so much of the mystery of God that will always remain beyond our comprehension. But, difficult though it is, we must believe that God is not immune to the agony of our world. As we shall discover in the course of our reflections, God suffers with his people; he makes himself vulnerable in the self-giving love of Jesus on the Cross; he accepts all human sorrow and pain into his very being. And so, we must not be so overwhelmed by our perception of God's omnipotence that we miss a heart of infinite love.

In Fulfilment: do we need God?

But, even when matters are going well, when we are experiencing the joy of love, the beauty of nature and the triumphant advance of technology, where is there room for God? In almost every area of human endeavour, whether it be in agriculture, in communication, in technology, in medicine, or in space exploration, there have been tremendous advances in human achievement. It would seem that, far from the heavens proclaiming the glory of God, they declare the glory of human progress and hold promise of still greater achievements within our grasp. Surely, we are well on the way to finding a less mysterious explanation of how the universe came to be, than the 'Lord'. We need look no further than our own powers in our search for self-understanding.

For many people, the above self-questionings don't constitute a problem at all. There are the apathetic people who couldn't care less whether there is a God or not. They see no need for God and have no sense of the importance of the question concerning God. There are others, by way of contrast, who possess a simplicity of heart, and see themselves and the world with the clarity of a child. Far from being a question, God is the most obvious fact there is. William James speaks of such people as being 'once born', people who seem to sail through life without experiencing anything that complicates their faith.[3] And finally, there are others who have gone through the doubts; they have experienced the 'dark night of the soul' and have risen to a tranquil faith. They now experience the calm after the storm. Theirs is not a simple, naive, superficial kind of faith; it is a mature faith, a faith which has experienced the problems of life and is now able to make its own the declaration of St Thomas: 'My Lord and my God'. Nothing, it would seem, could ever shake such faith again. They are, what William James would call, 'twice born people', not quite so cheerful, perhaps, as the 'once born people', but still confident that God will always enable them to keep going in a stormy and dangerous world.[4] But, for the rest of us, matters will continue to be a struggle. How does God make himself known to us?

A NATURAL OPENNESS TO THE MYSTERY OF GOD

As we have already mentioned, a fundamental tenet of our Christian faith is that we are made in the image and likeness of God. This means that there must be a fundamental connection between the being of God and our experience of life. If God wishes to make himself known and to share his love with us to the full, then, everything else must exist to make this possible. So it must be true to say that we are created in such a way as to be able to receive the love of God; indeed, in every heart there is a built-in yearning for God: 'You have made us for yourself, O Lord, and our heart can never rest until it rests in you'.[5]

In Creation

This is true, first of all, of creation itself. In the words of the poet Gerard Manley Hopkins: 'The World is charged with the grandeur of God: it will flame out, like shining from shook foil',[6] words echoed in John Newman's sermon 'The Invisible World' given in 1837:

> Let these be your thoughts, my brethren, especially in the spring season, when the whole face of nature is so rich and beautiful. Once only in the year, yet once, does the world which we see

show forth its hidden powers, and in a manner manifest itself. Then the leaves come out, and blossoms on the fruit trees and flowers; and the grass and corn spring up. There is a sudden rush and burst outwardly of that hidden life which God has lodged in the material world.

In Human Experience

Indeed, the mystery of God is not far from any of us, 'since it is in him that we live, and move, and exist' (Acts 17:28). In and through our varied experiences of life we are rooted in the ultimate mystery which embraces our minds and hearts. We become aware of the mystery in moments of silence, at times of joy and despair, in contemplating the beauty of creation. There is no escaping the presence of the mystery.

> 'Yahweh, you examine me and know me, you know if I am standing or sitting, you read my thoughts from far away, whether I walk or lie down, you are watching, you know every detail of my conduct . . . Where could I go to escape your spirit? where could I flee from your presence? If I climb the heavens, you are there; there too, if I lie in Sheol.
>
> Psalm 139; cf Catechism par. 28

Karl Rahner has described the presence of this mystery in the heart of everyone in the following terms:

Where someone experiences laughter or tears, bears responsibility, stands by the truth, breaks through the selfishness in his life with other people; where someone hopes against hope, faces the shallowness and stupidity of the daily rush and bustle with humour and patience, refusing to become embittered; where someone learns to be silent and in this inner silence lets the evil in his heart die rather than spread outwards; in a word, wherever someone lives as he would like to live, combatting his own selfishness and the continual temptation to inner despair – there is the event of grace.[7]

'Signals of Transcendence'

But it is Peter Berger, perhaps, who best describes what he refers to as 'signals of transcendence': ordinary experiences in life which nevertheless point to something greater – an ultimate reality – the presence of mystery. He speaks of the way in which a mother reassures her anxious child: 'Don't be frightened, everything will be all right.' Regardless of whether she is aware of it or not, she is saying it makes sense to trust. Her words of assurance to the child only really make sense because they point to another world in which love is not annihilated in death and where trust is fully justified. Another 'signal of transcendence' he describes is that of play – usually a joyful activity carried out in its own time scale. Time, as it were, seems to stand still, and in joyful play one recovers the innocence of childhood and steps into a world free of pain and death – into eternity. Another basic element of the human condition and a powerful 'signal of transcendence' is hope. It is through hope that we overcome difficulties of the here and now; it is through hope that we find meaning in the face of extreme suffering, even death itself. In fact it is because of hope that a 'no' to death is rooted in our very being. We refuse to capitulate before the inevitability of death and are brought to faith in another world.[8]

Experience alone remains ambiguous

However, the 'signals of transcendence', the various signs of the presence of mystery in and through our ordinary everyday experiences, will always remain ambiguous. How can we be sure about God? And if there is a God, does he really care about us? Is the mystery of life ultimately gracious to all that is within it? We can never be absolutely sure. In addition to our own selfishness and our own fears, there is the widespread experience of pain, as we have already mentioned, which seems to speak of the absence of God. He is not around when he is most needed. Nevertheless, there is a sureness, a profound conviction in faith, that a gracious God does embrace our life and will not let us go. Such a faith is able to recognise the word, so full of promise, that God himself speaks to us.

SEALED BY GOD'S COVENANT

God saw that it was good . . . (Genesis 1-3)

In the opening chapters of Genesis we have a marvellous confession of faith in a God who alone has created our world, has declared it to be good and is deeply concerned for it. Man and woman are made in the image of God; together they stand at the apex of all creation and are granted dominion over all that has been made. Indeed, God has called men and women to be with him as co-partners in creation and share with him his appreciation that 'it is very good'. The days when these pages of Genesis were written were dark days in the history of Israel, days of deportation and long exile from Palestine. She was at the very nadir of her existence. The writers of Genesis, therefore, were certainly realists. Nevertheless, they were able to penetrate the dark side of their experience of life and proclaim without ambiguity a song of hope in praise of the God whose hand spread out the heavens and laid the foundations of the earth. Such is the mark of those who are made in the image of God: who look evil in the face, who know what lies in every heart including their own, who can be battered by life, and yet are still able to declare that life is good. Such is the word contained in the moment of creation: the word of a God whose steadfast love endures for ever. There is never a time when God ceases to love us; his love is constant, forever (Catechism, par. 54).

Noah and the Rainbow Sign (Genesis 8-9)

The story of the Flood is one of the most important in the Bible. It begins with the sad observation that the earth is filled with violence which is an affront to God: 'Yahweh regretted having made human beings on earth and was grieved at heart' (Genesis 6:6-7). Noah, however, is a righteous man, a man who walks with God, and so in him God sees the possibility of a new beginning for all humankind. Because of Noah's righteousness God promises that he will never again destroy every human creature (Genesis 8:21). And when the rainbow appears in the clouds: 'I shall recall the Covenant between myself and you and every living creature . . . I shall see it and call to mind the eternal covenant between God and every living creature on earth, that is, all living things' (Genesis 9:15-16). God's promise is for everyone and that promise still holds good for us today (Catechism par. 56-58).

The Promises to Abraham (Genesis 12)

Once again, however, the human story takes a turn for the worse. The people rebelled and wandered far away from God, building for themselves the tower of Babel, a monument to human pride (Genesis 11:1-10). True to form, God begins again, this time by choosing Abraham, from Ur of the Chaldees (in present day Iraq). First of all he changes his name from Abram to Abraham, which means 'the father of a multitude of nations'. Sarah is his wife and, we are told, 'she was barren; she had no child' (Genesis 11:30). God asks Abraham to leave his country, his family, and his father's house and then proceeds to make him a series of promises: 'I shall make you a great nation, I shall bless you and make your name famous; you are to be a blessing! I shall bless those who bless you and shall curse those who curse you, and all clans on earth will bless themselves by you (Genesis 12:1-3). It is in fulfilment of these promises that God will not be thwarted, neither by old age nor barrenness. The child that was to come from the barren womb of Sarah was to be the beginning of the people from whom will come Jesus of Nazareth: 'Yahweh treated Sarah as he had said, and did what he had promised her' (Genesis 21:1). God will not be frustrated by human failure or by disbelief; he is determined to bless his people (cf Catechism par. 59-61).

The Formation of the People Israel

God's determination to bless all peoples gradually comes to a focus in the covenant he made with the people of Israel. 'You have seen for yourselves what I did to the Egyptians and how I carried you away on eagles' wings and brought you to me. So now, if you are really prepared to obey me and keep my covenant, you, out of all peoples, shall be my personal possession, for the whole world is mine. For me you shall be a kingdom of priests, a holy nation' (Exodus 19:4-6). He would be their God and they would be his people, and he would never fail them. This covenant would give them a permanent basis for hope in their survival, growth, and future existence. Apart from their relationship to God they are 'No-people', a lost people without hope and without life. Their God was a God of everlasting love: 'Yahweh, Yahweh, God of tenderness and compassion, slow to anger, rich in faithful love and constancy' (Exodus 34:6). And again in Deuteronomy: 'Yahweh set his heart on you and chose you, not because you were the most numerous of all peoples – for indeed you were the smallest of all – but because he loved you and meant to keep the oath which he swore to your ancestors: that was why Yahweh brought you out with his mighty hand and redeemed you from the place of slave-labour, from the power of Pharaoh King of Egypt' (Deuteronomy 7:7). God was utterly dependable and even when he is angry it only lasts a moment: 'Ephraim, how could I part with you? Israel, how could I give you up? . . . My heart within me is overwhelmed, fever grips my inmost being . . . for . . . I am the Holy One in your midst and I shall not come to you in anger' (Hosea 11:8-9; cf Catechism pars. 62-64).

Jesus Christ: the Beloved Son

God's relationship with his people turned out to be a turbulent love affair. And when they tried to live without him, God began to focus upon a people within a people, who would be faithful to their election and vocation. This small group of faithful ones became known as the Remnant, from whom Jesus Christ is eventually to emerge. It is in Christ that God's purpose for all is to find fulfilment. At his Transfiguration, Christ is spoken of as the Chosen One. He represents all before God. In Christ we are the heirs of the promises given long ago to Abraham, Noah and Israel. Now we know that our God is faithful. He loves to the end and in that final hour upon the Cross our destiny is settled. From the very beginning, God had intended to utter this final Word. Before God ever uttered that first word of creation, 'Let there be light', he was determined to make his home with us in the person of his Son Jesus Christ (cf Catechism pars. 65-68).

OUR RESPONSE IN FAITH: I BELIEVE

A Matter of Trust

The only appropriate response to the Word of God, spoken from the first moment of creation and finally in his Son Jesus Christ, is faith, believing in one's heart that God is good, is always on our side, and that we are, each of us, his very special possession, treasured and prized. It provides us with a centre of gravity and a reason for living in a world of challenge and adversity. It enables us to realise that there is always the possibility of a new beginning; it does not give way to self-pity but reacts positively to all manner of adversity, seeing it neither as waste nor as punishment but as opportunity. When we believe in God, we see reality as God saw it when he created it; when we believe in God we begin to see that it is good, that with God all things are possible.

Models of Faith

• Abraham: 'Our father in faith' (Genesis 22)

Abraham is described as 'our father in faith' – a model for all believers. His faith was sorely tested: he was required to leave his own country and to travel to an unknown land. Now he is commanded by God to make the ultimate sacrifice of his own son, Isaac, upon whom all the future blessings of God depended. It would seem to be an absurd demand, and yet Abraham has sufficient faith to accept and say 'Yes'. We know the end of the story: Abraham's hand is stayed and Isaac is unbound. But what is the point? In that moment, Abraham believed to the utmost that God would provide. In surrendering his son, Isaac, Abraham died to self and placed his total trust in God. The future belongs to God and all the blessings on the world are now secure (cf Romans 11:18; and also Catechism pars. 145-147).

• Mary: The woman of faith (Luke 1:48-50)

The Letter to the Hebrews speaks of many heroes of faith in the Old Testament, 'but they did not receive what was promised, since God had made provision for us to have something better, and they were not to receive perfection except with us . . . Let us keep our eyes fixed on Jesus, who leads us in our faith and brings it to perfection' (Hebrews 11:39-40). Such perfection is particularly evident in the person of Mary, the Mother of Jesus. It was of her that her cousin, Elizabeth, said: 'Blessed is she who believed that the promise made her by the Lord would be fulfilled' (Luke 1:45). It is the faith by which she received the Word of God that makes her by the power of the Spirit the Mother of God: 'Let what you have said be done to me' (Luke 1:38). Because of her faith, she conceived the Word, she gave the Word flesh, and the world received its Saviour. From the moment of his conception, as she bore him in her womb, as she gave him birth, as she fostered him and saw him grow up, as she witnessed his death upon the cross, there was always so much she did not understand. Indeed, there were times when relations between Jesus and Mary seemed to be quite strained (cf Mark 3:21; Luke 2:48-49; John 2:4). Nevertheless, she remained faithful to him to the end, a model of true discipleship (Luke 1:48-50; 2:19,39; cf Catechism pars. 148-149; 963-972).

• *Jesus: the Way of faith*

We normally speak of believing *in* Jesus, the person on whom our faith depends from start to finish. Nevertheless, it is appropriate to speak of Jesus, during the course of his earthly life, as a man of faith. Indeed, it would be impossible to speak of Jesus as fully human if we denied that he needed to have faith. And so, at the beginning of his life, we are told that 'Jesus increased in wisdom, in stature, and in favour with God and with people' (Luke 2:52). Throughout his public ministry, Jesus expressed his total dependence upon the Father who sent him, the Father with whom he spent so much time in prayer, and yet the Father who did not intervene. Nowhere did Jesus experience visible help from the one whose cause he had so much at heart. On the contrary, Jesus was frequently conscious of an inner conflict arising from the utter silence of the one whom he was accustomed to call his Father. Only this can explain the struggle of Jesus in the Garden of Gethsemane and the cry of abandonment from the Cross. A text which expresses so well this faith-experience of Jesus is to be found in the Letter to the Hebrews: 'During his life on earth, he offered up prayer and entreaty, with loud cries and with tears, to the one who had the power to save him from death, and, winning a hearing by his reverence, he learnt obedience, Son though he was, through his sufferings' (Hebrews 5: 7-9). Not only, therefore, must we believe *in* Jesus, but we must also believe *like* Jesus.

The essence of faith, then, is to trust in God as utterly trustworthy, and so to know that we are safe, that we are all right, whatever happens to us, however unsafe we may be, however much things may go wrong. Trusting in God means that God is the very foundation of our life. Once we stand on that ground, then faith takes root and begins to grow, and we begin to realise possibilities undreamed of. In the words of Jesus: 'If your faith is the size of a mustard seed you will say to this mountain: "Move from here to there" and it will move; nothing will be impossible for you' (Matthew 17:20).

Essential Characteristics of Faith

• A gift of God

Faith is first and foremost a gift of God. It flows from the presence of the Spirit of God within us. Centuries ago Jeremiah proclaimed the words of Yahweh in the following terms: 'I will put my law within them and write it on their hearts . . . all will know me from the least to the greatest' (Jeremiah 31:33-34). And again in the prophecy of Ezekiel: 'I will put my spirit in you and I will see to it that you will follow my laws and keep all the commands I have given you' (Ezekiel 36:25-27). These prophecies find their fulfilment in the New Testament which describes the presence of the Spirit of Christ within us as an inner illumination, opening our hearts to faith in the Gospel: 'The God who said, "Out of darkness the light shall shine" is the same God who made his light shine in our hearts, to bring us the knowledge of God's glory shining in the face of Christ' (2 Corinthians 4:4-6). And when Peter confessed that Jesus was the Christ, the Son of the living God, Jesus replied, 'You are a happy man! Because it was not flesh and blood that revealed this to you but my Father in heaven' (Matthew 16:17; Catechism par. 153).

• A human action

Although faith is a gift of God and only possible through the workings of the Holy Spirit within us, it is nevertheless an authentically human action. Indeed, acts of faith are commonplace in everyday life. When people entrust their secrets to friends, business affairs to solicitors, place their lives into the hands of doctors, they are making acts of faith and entrusting themselves to them. But these pale into insignificance when compared with the act of faith two human beings make in each other on their wedding day. It is an act of faith which moves each to give to the other all that is precious and intimate within them. It is a gift which makes great demands and calls for the acceptance of great responsibilities. It is a gift which makes for a much wider and deeper experience of life. And so, within human experience, we are accustomed to that kind of response which God asks of us when Jesus says: 'Do not let your hearts be troubled. You trust in God, trust also in me' (John 14:1; Catechism pars. 154-155).

• *Acceptance of the hiddeness of God*

An essential aspect of our faith is that God remains in 'unapproachable light' (1 Timothy 6:16), whom not even the heavens can contain (2 Chronicles 6:18). And so we can never wholly grasp the mystery of God. God is not God unless He is both present and absent to us who are his creatures. From beginning to end this will always remain the constant paradox: 'I am your God, you are my people'; 'Why, O Lord, do you hide your face?'; 'I am with you always'; 'My God, my God, why have you forsaken me?' Even in human experience, two people deeply in love realise more and more that there is always an element of the other which is inaccessible, always beyond the grasp of the one who loves. If this is true of human relationships, it is so much more true of God's love for us and our love for him where we meet the paradox of presence and absence in its most acute and final form. Such an experience calls for great faith because it means that true believers who trust in God know that they are still held in God's hands, even though there is no help that they can touch or feel, and, in utmost emptiness, will not let go of his hand. It is in this context that E.Schillebeeckx speaks of prayer as a game of hide and seek.[9]

• *Guarantee of our hope*

Faith in what has happened to Jesus is the guarantee of our continuing hope, of an eventual end to darkness, and of the promise that, in spite of present appearances, all will finally be well. His whole life speaks to us of a life that knows no bounds and considers no situation beyond redemption. He faced up to his own death with great courage, knowing that he would have to experience the full horror of it. And from the depths of despair and nothingness, in his resurrection he has given us the pledge of new hope and new life. In faith, we know that the life of the world is in good hands. God has good things in store for all of us.

Witness of Faith

During his public ministry, Jesus warned against those who honoured him only with lip-service, while their hearts were far from him (Mark 7:6). We need to remember those words when reflecting upon the opening words of the Creed. We believe in God and not simply that God exists. This means that our confession of faith must be reflected both in our commitment to prayer and in our pattern of behaviour. As we know only too well from human experience, love and friendship can only survive if sustained by looks, gestures and words. Love must find expression through bodily gestures if it is to bear fruit in deep and lasting happiness. The same is true of our relationship with God.

• *Commitment to prayer*

Prayer should be the natural overflow of our life of faith. If we know who and what we really are, human beings created in such a way as to be able to receive the love of God, then we should not be able to help ourselves bursting forth in prayer of praise and thanksgiving. If we experience the goodness and glory of God deep within us then we shall always want to praise him. Examples of such prayer fill the pages of the scriptures, especially the Psalms many of which are hymns of praise: 'Bless Yahweh, my soul, from the depths of my being, his holy name; Bless Yahweh, my soul, never forget all his acts of kindness' (Psalm 103:1-3).

The same is inevitably true of prayer in the New Testament. The faith of the mother of Jesus naturally overflows into her Magnificat: 'My soul proclaims the greatness of the Lord, and my spirit rejoices in God my Saviour'(Luke 2:46); and Jesus himself prays: 'I bless you, Father, Lord of heaven and of earth, for hiding these things from the learned and the clever and revealing them to little children' (Luke 10:21).

All this prayer is gathered together in our celebration of Eucharist, the principal focus of our thanksgiving and our praise of God: 'We come to you, Father, with praise and thanksgiving, through Jesus Christ your Son'. Because of our faith, praise and thanksgiving should be as instinctive to the Christian heart as breathing. In the words of St Paul: 'In all your prayer and entreaty keep praying in the Spirit on every possible occasion. Never get tired of staying awake to pray for all God's holy people' (Ephesians 6:18).

• *A sign to the world*

If we are truly a prayerful people, filled with the Spirit of God, then, we shall instinctively share with others what we ourselves have received. This means that we shall only touch the hearts of others by knowing God: possessing a deeply rooted conviction of being totally accepted and cherished by God as Father; recognising Jesus as the Lord of our life; and experiencing the Spirit praying within, bringing alive the love that comes from the Father and Son. But, as we look upon the world, broken by suffering of every kind, we can be overcome by a feeling of helplessness. Each of us has our own particular concerns of work, mortgage, examinations, bringing up children, and the cost of living. How can we respond in a practical way to the many global issues that cry out for our attention: world poverty, world hunger and starvation, world inflation, over population, pollution, the arms race?

In speaking at Coventry of the need for world peace, Pope John Paul II has pointed the way forward when faced with seemingly insuperable problems:

> 'The cathedral of peace is built of many small stones. Each person has to become a stone in that beautiful edifice . . . Mistrust and division between nations begin in the hearts of individuals. Work for peace starts when we listen to the urgent call of Christ: "Repent and believe in the Gospel"'.[10]

NOTES
1 W Steele, *Can We Be Sure About God?* (UNI Tape 1978)
2 Macbeth, Act 5, Scene v.
3 William James, *The Varieties of Religious Experience* (Fontana Library 1960) p. 94.
4 William James op. cit. p. 172
5 Confessions of St Augustine 1, 1, 1 (cf catechism pars. 27-30)
6 God's Grandeur in the Oxford Authors: Gerard Manley Hopkins, (Oxford 1986), p. 258
7 Karl Rahner, *Theological Investigations, vol. 5* (DLT 1966), p. 8
8 Peter L Berger, *Rumour of Angels* (Penguin 1969)
9 E Schillebeeckx, *Christ* (SCM 1980), p. 816
10 *The Pope in Britain* (St Paul Publications, 1982), p. 9

FURTHER READING
Catechism of the Catholic Church: pars. 26-95, 142-165
Berger, Peter, *Rumour of Angels* (Penguin 1969)
Lash, Nicholas, *Believing Three Ways in One God* (SCM 1992)
O'Hanlon, Joseph, *The Dance of the Merrymakers* (St Paul Publications 1991)
Smith, Aelred, *Why Should I Read the Bible?* (Uniscript 1979)

CHAPTER TWO

THE FATHER OF OUR LORD JESUS CHRIST

A PUZZLING DOCTRINE

All-Too Familiar

We are accustomed to speak of the mystery of the triune God as the innermost heart of the Christian faith. It is part of the inherited package of Christian belief: we frequently make the sign of the cross 'in the name of the Father, and of the Son, and of the Holy Spirit'; we are baptised into the name of the triune God, marriages are sealed with his blessing, and the dead are committed to his infinite mercy. At every turn, we make that simple profession of faith in the triune God which we find at key points in the New Testament. St Matthew's Gospel concludes with the risen Lord sending his followers to make disciples of all nations baptising them in the name of the Father and of the Son and of the Holy Spirit (Matthew 28:19). And Paul rounds off his second letter to the Corinthians with a blessing that is now a familiar greeting at the beginning of Mass: 'The grace of our Lord Jesus Christ and the love of God and the fellowship of the Holy Spirit be with you all' (2 Corinthians 13:14). If we are at home in the practices and beliefs of the Catholic Church, then perhaps the most familiar article of the Creed is the doctrine of God as Trinity – as the communion of Father, Son, and Holy Spirit, into whose love we are all invited.

Nevertheless, Puzzling

And yet, despite its familiarity, most of us can find it a puzzling doctrine, especially when we reflect upon the way in which it has been expounded down the ages. What, for example, are we to make of the Creed of St Athanasius?

> 'Eternal Father, eternal Son, eternal Holy Spirit; and yet, not three Eternals but one Eternal . . . One Father, not three Fathers; one Son, not three Sons; one Holy Spirit, not three Holy Spirits. And in this Trinity there is no before or after, no more or less, but all three co-eternal persons are equal with each other so that in everything we must venerate unity in Trinity and Trinity in unity. Whoever wants to be saved must think this of the Trinity.'

We may be pardoned for thinking it must be somewhat difficult to be saved! One can sympathise with a certain Bishop Pyke who used to say that the age-old doctrine of the Trinity should be abandoned since it is a stumbling block to the spread of Christianity. As he once quipped: 'The Muslims offer one God and three wives; we offer three Gods and one wife. No wonder Christianity is losing out in Africa.'[1]

An Essential Doctrine?

How many Christians today, when trying to speak of the faith by which they live, are able to speak of their understanding of the Trinity? There are, we say, three persons in one God. Must we then be reduced to silence and simply accept this formula 'on faith', or must we ask further how God can, at the same time, be both one and three? Many of us, I suspect, assume that God is in some way three people because, within human experience, this is the only way in which we can make sense of the term 'person'. But our God is one God and so our understanding of 'person' as applied to God will need to be modified, adjusted and corrected if it is not to compromise our recognition of the oneness of God. Hence, the speculation down the ages, much of it quite unintelligible, without much relevance to the life and prayer of ordinary

Christians. In the words of one writer: 'It has become a toy for theologians rather than a joy for believers'.[2] We must ask ourselves why it is that the most all-embracing mystery of our faith has suffered such a fate.

ISOLATION OF TRINITARIAN DOCTRINE

Focus upon God's Inner Life

Beginning in the Middle Ages, a significant shift of emphasis took place within the Western Church whereby theological attention was focussed upon the threefold internal structure of God. The danger of this is obvious. Talk about God, isolated from the historical circumstances in which God made his name known as Father, Son and Holy Spirit, seemed to be a matter of pure speculation; an attempt by philosophical thinking to explain to itself the hidden processes which take place in God. On this fundamental aspect of Christian faith, much of theology no longer corresponded to the Christian experience of God. As a result, there emerged a split between theologians and worshippers, a split between the highly speculative theorising about God's inner life and the great movements of devotion which grew up in compensation. These had little relation to the classical explanation of the Trinity and, instead, sought to reflect on what it means to participate in the life of God through Jesus Christ in the Spirit. Unfortunately, much of theology perplexed the mind but never touched the heart (cf Catechism par. 236).

Emphasis upon the Unity of God

Within our tradition, too, practically all the emphasis has been placed upon the unity of the divine nature which all three persons share in common. Already, by the time of St Augustine, it was a firmly established principle that whatever God does that is not God is done, indivisibly, by all three persons. And so the answer to the question 'Who creates the world?' is 'God' and we are accustomed to speak of 'God becoming human'. In the words of Karl Rahner, 'Christians are, in their practical life, almost mere monotheists'.[3] This way of speaking, of course, is perfectly orthodox; but more needs to be said of the distinct relationships we enjoy with Father, Son and Spirit if this central aspect of our Christian faith is not to be relegated to the margins of most people's piety, thought and practice.

We have also tended to refer to God as 'he' and, in that way, to see God as a single solitary being, as a monarch, as a master, as severe. We know only too well from experience how difficult it is to relate to such a God or to pray to such a God or even to live with such a God. The prevailing attitude of so many has been that of fear, carrying within them an impersonal god, a god of stone, unfriendly and unforgiving, who must at all costs be placated. We have all been touched in varying degrees by such a misconception of God and so we know immediately what is meant when we say of someone in power: 'he thinks he is God!' It reflects little or none of that wholly personal experience of the relationship of Christ to the Father which he sought to share with us in the Spirit. 'Anyone who loves me will keep my word, and my Father will love him, and we shall come to him and make a home in him' (John 14:23).

Neglect of the Holy Spirit

The Holy Spirit has long been the forgotten person of the Trinity. This was a criticism voiced repeatedly by bishops of the Orthodox tradition at the Second Vatican Council and, as a general criticism, it seems well founded. We traditionally assumed that grace could not make its presence felt in our conscious personal lives; we lost our sense of Christian fellowship and concentrated almost exclusively on our private relationship with God; and we were suspicious of all spiritual movements of enthusiasm. In more recent times, however, we are beginning to experience a new presence of the Spirit within the Church who alone can bring alive the love that comes from the Father and the Son. And so it is only in the Spirit that the risen Lord can be present to us; it is because of the Spirit that the Gospel is no longer a dead letter but the power of life; it is by the Spirit that the Church becomes a communion of believers made one by the Father, Son and Holy Spirit; it is in the Spirit that our liturgy is truly an occasion for celebration. Without such an experience of the Spirit of God in our lives, the Trinity will forever remain a matter of pure speculation.

A Word of Caution

In our criticism of the past, however, it must never be suggested that talk about God must come naturally to us. If we find it easy to say certain things of God, the chances are that, when we say them, we lose sight of God; and even when we say things legitimately of God, we must always do so in 'fear and trembling', in recognition that what we say is quite beyond us. We must be mindful of the Jews who scarcely dared to utter the word 'God' at all. The more deeply they learned to know him, the more unutterable became his name and the more inconceivable he became himself. Likewise, St Augustine, who spent twenty years writing on the Trinity, said, 'If you think you have understood something, then it was certainly not God'.[4] And finally, St Thomas Aquinas too was most concerned to protect the mystery of God: 'One thing about God remains completely unknown in this life, namely, what God is'.[5]

Nevertheless, this God, who remains beyond all human knowing, has come close to us in the flesh and blood of Jesus Christ to be seen and touched. In Jesus, God addresses us as Father and challenges us to entrust ourselves to him unconditionally. This demand is justified with the testimony that God has given of his love for the world (John 3:16). We are able to draw near the God 'whose home is in unapproachable light, whom no human being has seen or is able to see' (1 Timothy 6:16), 'in boldness and confidence through our faith in Jesus Christ' (Ephesians 3:12). We must accept the path which God himself offers us into the mystery of his eternal love.

GOD MAKES HIMSELF KNOWN IN JESUS
THROUGH THE POWER OF THE SPIRIT

A Lesson from the Early Christian Community

The early Christian community arrived at the formula 'three persons in one God' by reflecting upon the way in which God had chosen to make himself known in Jesus Christ and in the Spirit. They believed that God had become human in the person of Jesus Christ and that, furthermore, he still dwelt with the community and guided it. The aim of theologians during this period was far more practical than might seem on the surface. What they were concerned to say was that in Jesus Christ we and God are truly reconciled. They did not believe this to be possible unless God came to where we are. In Jesus God has given himself totally – Jesus is none other than the Word of God made flesh. This is what lies behind the whole teaching of those early Councils of the Church. At the Council of Nicaea in 325, the Church affirmed that the Lord Jesus Christ was 'one in substance with the Father' and at the Council of Chalcedon in 451 that Jesus Christ was 'truly God and truly man'. It is only on the basis of such faith that we can acknowledge Jesus as our Saviour, reconciling us to God.

But this reconciliation was not something which took place once for all in the person of Jesus Christ; it was carried on within the community through the work of the Holy Spirit. And so, once again, theologians used surprisingly practical arguments when they were arguing in favour of the divinity of the Holy Spirit: we know the Holy Spirit must be God because it is the function of the Holy Spirit to draw us into communion with God. At the Council of Constantinople in 381, therefore, it was defined that the Spirit too is 'one in substance with the Father and the Son'. The Spirit is none other than God himself. Only in this way could they do justice to their own experience of the Spirit so well expressed in the writings of St Paul to the Romans.

> 'All who are guided by the Spirit of God are sons
> of God; for what you received was not the spirit

of slavery to bring you back into fear; you received the spirit of adoption, enabling us to cry out, "Abba, Father!" The Spirit himself joins with our spirit to bear witness that we are children of God. And if we are children, then we are heirs, heirs of God and joint-heirs with Christ, provided that we share his suffering, so as to share his glory.' (Romans 8:15)

When, therefore, they were formulating their faith in the Trinity, the Fathers of the Church were not interested in abstract formulae, but in understanding the mystery of our salvation in Christ and defending it against misunderstandings. The impulse which drove them to these explorations was anything but a mania for speculation. The reason for their unwavering faith in the divinity of the Son and the Spirit was their conviction that if the Son and the Spirit are not really God, then we have no share in that communion with God. In other words, their understanding of God was based upon their experience of God as he had made himself known to them in Jesus Christ and the Spirit.

We, too, must adopt this perspective; and so it is for this reason that it is best to reflect upon the mystery of the Trinity in the light of the event of Christ upon the cross. There, above all, we come to know our God, Father, Son and Holy Spirit, as a God of love. (For a technical presentation of the Church's understanding of the Trinity cf Catechism pars. 249-260).

The Mystery of the Trinity and the Event of the Cross

In all Christian Churches, the cross has become the sign which distinguishes them from other religions and modes of belief. At the same time, what is distinctive about the Christian understanding of God is the doctrine of the Trinity. If this is so, then, surely, there must be an essential connection between these two special features of Christianity: faith in the crucified Jesus and in the triune God. After all, how often do we make the sign of the cross and say: 'In the name of the Father, and of the Son, and of the Holy Spirit'?

● *Jesus' relationship to the Father*

Our starting point must be the experience of Jesus' communion with God whom he dared to address as 'Father': 'Everything has been entrusted to me by my Father; and no one knows who the Son is except the Father, and who the Father is except the Son and those to whom the Son chooses to reveal him' (Luke 10:22). And again: 'In all truth I tell you, by himself the Son can do nothing; he can do only what he sees the Father doing: and whatever the Father does the Son does too. For the Father loves the Son and shows him everything he himself does'. (John 5:19-21). Jesus is saying to us that his Father, Creator of heaven and earth, is the one whose will he does perfectly; every word he speaks, every work he does, is the Father's word and work. This God whom he addresses as 'Father' is the one who sustains him in all that he is asked to undergo.

It is certainly a communion of intimacy and familiarity but it is far removed from sentimentality. It involves a great deal: 'Father, if you are willing, take this cup away from me. Nevertheless, let your will be done not mine' (Luke 22:42). And so, in his response to Philip, who asked to see the Father, Jesus says: 'Have I been with you all this time, Philip, and you still do not know me? Anyone who has seen me has seen the Father. Do you not believe that I am in the Father and the Father is in me?' (John 14:8-10). It is only in the context of this communion of life between the Father and the Son that we begin to understand the event of the cross (cf Catechism par. 240).

● *The event of the cross*

According to Ss. Paul and Mark, Jesus himself was abandoned by the Father and died with a cry of godforsakenness. In the words of St Paul: 'If God is for us, who can be against us? Since he did not spare his own Son, but gave him up for the sake of all of us, then can we not expect that with him he will freely give us all his gifts?' (Romans 8:31). And again, in even stronger terms: 'For our sake, God made the sinless one a victim for sin' (2 Corinthians 5:21); and, 'Christ redeemed us from the curse of the Law by being cursed for our sake, since Scripture says: "Anyone hanged is accursed"' (Galations 3:13). St Paul, in these words, wishes to express in the strongest possible terms the extent of the Son's mission from the Father: he is sent to experience fully that sickness unto death which is the lot of everyone who has strayed away from God. The God whom Jesus had dared to call 'Father' has suddenly become silent. The Father with whom he had experienced such a communion of intimacy now seems sadly absent.

But if St Paul and St John speak of Jesus as the Father's *only* Son, the experience of Jesus 'being abandoned' and 'not being spared' must also involve the Father himself. God the Father cannot be indifferent to the suffering and death of his only-begotten Son. Far from being absent, therefore, the moment when Jesus dies upon the cross is the moment when the Father is most present. In the surrender of the Son, the Father also surrenders himself. And so Jesus does not die because compelled to do so by the Father; rather, together with the Father he freely gives himself up. Jesus consciously and willingly walked the way of the Cross and was in no way overtaken by death as by an evil, unfortunate, fate. And so we read in St John's Gospel: '(The prince of this world) has no power over me, but the world must recognise that I love the Father and that I act just as the Father commanded. Come now, let us go' (John 14:31). It is important to know that both the Father and the Son are involved in this act of 'delivering-up' since it expresses a deep community of will between Father and Son at the point of their seeming deepest separation. Jesus dies not out of fear, but out of love for his Father.

• *The outpouring of the spirit in the resurrection*

It is because of the resurrection that we know the Father received that final prayer of Jesus: 'Father, into your hands I commend my spirit'. It is now that this mutual 'surrender' upon the cross can be described in terms of love: 'For this is how God loved the world: he gave his only Son, so that everyone who believes in him may not perish but may have eternal life' (John 3:16). And in the first letter of St John, we read simply 'God is love' (1 John 4:16). God exists for us as love in the event of the cross. This is so because what proceeds from this event of the cross between the Father and the Son is the Spirit, the inner life of God, poured out for all of us and filling our hearts and our world with his presence. There is no outside of the Trinity; the love of the Father, the Son and the Holy Spirit is wide enough to embrace the whole world and, indeed, the whole of creation.

If we, as Christians, are to speak of God, then, we must tell the story of Jesus as the story of God; made known upon the cross is the inner heart of God. We know that God is not a loner, not remote, not self-absorbed. God is totally personal in whom there is life, activity, giving and receiving, speaking and answering, total interchange, heart to heart, person to person, the glory of answered love. There is only one life that Jesus knew, one of total intimacy with the Father through the power of the Spirit. Because of the cross, we know that this is the life he wants for us. That life of God touches every thought and movement of the world and of the human heart; it is nothing less than the breath of God which sustains all things in steadfast love.

CREATED IN THE IMAGE AND LIKENESS OF GOD

Male and Female 'She' Created Them

The notion of God as 'Father' is becoming increasingly problematic today, especially since it seems to suggest that only masculine imagery can be used appropriately of God. But, as we have already mentioned, when speaking of God we must exercise caution and recognise the limitations of language. No symbol, no metaphor, however privileged as in the case of 'Father', can exhaust the richness of the mystery of God. Indeed, every statement we make about God must be negated. And so, we speak of God as father, king, shepherd, and so on; but almost in the same breath, we have to say that God is not a father, king, and shepherd, as we are, both because of our sinfulness and of our limitations. We also need to remember that when we speak of God as 'Father', it is not in distinction from God as 'Mother'.[6] Rather, it is to emphasise God as personal; it is a term of intimacy that was such a characteristic feature of the life and prayer of Jesus. There is no reason, therefore, why the symbol of 'Father' should be removed from the centre of Christian faith. Nevertheless, it does need to be modified and enriched by other symbols, not least amongst them being that of God as 'Mother' (cf Catechism par. 239).

• *The 'Fatherhood' of God in the Old Testament*

Within the Old Testament, God is described as 'Father' only eleven times and never invoked as such in prayer. Masculine imagery, on the other hand, is widely used and this could mean that we fail to notice important passages in which God is depicted in maternal terms. Examples can be found in the prophecy of Isaiah where Israel relates to God as one who conceives and brings the people to birth, suckles and feeds them, comforts them as a mother, and provides clothes to cover their nakedness (Isaiah 42:14; 49:15; 66:13). Another example can be found in the prophecy of Hosea, where the imagery is most certainly that of a mother and child.

> 'When Israel was a child I loved him, and I called my son out of Egypt. But the more I called, the further they went away from me . . . I myself taught Ephraim to walk, I myself took them by the arm . . . I was like someone lifting an infant to his cheek, and that I bent down to feed him.'
> (Hosea 11:1-4)

These female metaphors accomplish something that male metaphors on their own cannot: the image of God carrying Israel and giving birth in pain, of suckling Israel at the breast, are profound expressions for both men and women of the experience of relating to a deeply compassionate God. Short of saying that God possesses a womb, the Bible does say that 'Yahweh bears Israel from its conception to old age'.

• *Jesus calls God 'Abba'*

The New Testament does not contain specific maternal imagery of God. At its heart, of course, lies Jesus' preferred title for God as 'Father'. Nowhere does Jesus invoke God in prayer except by this title and he teaches his disciples to pray 'Our Father'. But the Father to whom Jesus prays is not a stern autocrat but a loving parent who agonises over the lost child and runs to meet him with joy at his return. In the words of one writer: 'Of all the models for God (that Jesus could have used) – judge, teacher, healer, and so on – none is closer to that of 'mother' than 'father' is . . . without actually saying 'God is our Mother' there is no closer preparation for it than saying 'God is our Father'.[7]

In later Christian tradition, Jesus himself is spoken of as a Mother. And so St Anselm speaks of Jesus as a Mother because he gives birth to souls and because he nurses and nourishes the newborn Christian; for Julian of Norwich, we feed on Jesus in the Eucharist as a baby feeds upon its mother; and a favourite passage of the Mystics is Matthew 23:37 where Jesus is likened to a hen gathering chicks under her wing.

• *Spirit: feminine principle*

The Spirit has frequently (although, as we have seen, not exclusively) been represented as the feminine principle within God. The biblical roots of the idea seem to lie in the use of the bird imagery in connection with the Spirit, especially that of a mother-bird hovering. This is seen within Christian tradition in the appearance of the Spirit as a dove at the baptism of Jesus. John 3:5 speaks of our being born of the Spirit and this is developed amongst the Eastern Fathers in terms of the Spirit as Mother: 'The Spirit is our Mother, because the Paraclete, the Comforter, will comfort as a mother her child (Isaiah 66:13) and because the believers are reborn out of the Spirit and are thus children of the mysterious Mother, the Spirit (John 3:3)'.[8]

At the heart of our experience of God is the experience of rebirth, unmerited love, security, compassion, forgiveness and service. All these experiences are central to Christian faith and it is difficult, if not impossible, to find better metaphors than the feminine ones for embodying them.[9]

The Involvement of God with his People

Traditional theology has for a long time been unable to do justice to the involvement of God with his people because of its one-sided insistence upon the 'immutability' of God. At its heart, this doctrine speaks of the faithfulness of God whose face is always turned towards us and who never changes his mind. In contrast to our moodiness, God is constant. In contrast to our fickleness, God keeps faith. In contrast to the transitoriness of everything, God abides forever. 'Your faithful love towers to heaven, your constancy to the clouds' (Psalm 57:10). But so great was the concern to deny any change in God which might denote imperfection, that God was presented as one immune to suffering and tragedy. It was felt that feelings could not be appropriately ascribed to God.

In the words of Bonhoeffer, however: 'Only a God who suffers can save'.[10] If God is love, then, he cannot possibly express that love in a world of misery without being affected by that misery. If the love of God is to be credible to the starving peoples of the world and the countless victims of war, poverty, and tragedy of one kind or another, then God must be affected in his very being by such suffering. In the words of Moltmann: 'A God who is incapable of suffering is a being who cannot be involved. Suffering and injustice do not affect him. And because he is so insensitive, he cannot be affected or shaken by anything. He cannot weep, for he has no tears. But the one who cannot suffer cannot love either'.[11] As we have seen already, however, the story of Jesus is none other than the story of God.

'It is not good that man should be alone' (Genesis 2:18)

Being made in the image and likeness of God means that the human heart, our heart, has received the divine impress, the divine signature. That is why the deepest ache of the human heart is for love. We want to be loved, first of all, as someone special, someone of value in our own eyes as well as in the eyes of others. We want to be ourselves, different from everyone else. Such a desire, such a love and respect for oneself, is confirmed by Jesus as the starting-point and, indeed, measure of the love that we must have for one another (cf Luke 10:25-27).

Emphasis upon the individual, however, can give rise to individualism and competitiveness, which has little respect for others, and seeks to grow by grabbing, snatching and keeping. Individual freedom can mean 'the right to do whatever one wants', often at the expense of others. Life can entail the survival of the fittest.

But, as John Donne wrote many years ago: 'No man is an island'. As individuals we must want to belong to something more than ourselves, to make relationships with others, to be part of a community. Our sense of identity is important, but so too is our sense of belonging. There should be no competition here. What I think of as *my* life is never just mine. It can only reach full development in relationship with other people. If we want to feel at home in the world, then, we can only do so through others.

The mystery of the Trinity holds the key. The Father's love comes to us in the particular person of Jesus Christ, at a particular time, in a particular place. When we look upon Jesus, we look upon one of us, a person like ourselves in the weakness of flesh and blood. No matter whether we are rich or poor, sick or healthy, no matter what our race, or creed, or colour, we are children of God, our Father, and brothers and sisters of Jesus Christ, and can be sure of our value and dignity.

But Jesus brought with him, too, the power of the Spirit of God to transform us into a community, where we would be free to be human and feel at home; a community shot through with love, united by love, breathing love, in which no one, however poor and miserable, should be bereft of hope and affection. This challenging ideal finds tremendous expression in the writings of St Paul.

> 'For as with the human body which is a unity although it has many parts – all the parts of the body, though many, still making up one single body – so it is with Christ . . . the parts are many but the body is one. The eye cannot say to the hand, "I have no need of you" . . . each part (must) be equally concerned for all the others.' (1 Corinthians 12:12)

NOTES

1 cited by Peter de Rosa, *Come, Holy Spirit* (Fontana 1975), p. 21
2 Walter J Burghardt, *Sir, We Would Like to See Jesus* (Paulist Press 1982), p. 151
3 Karl Rahner, *Theological Investigations* vol 4 (DLT 1966), p. 79
4 cited by Lawrence Cantwell, *The Theology of the Trinity* (Mercier Press 1969), p. 55
5 cited by John Courtney Murray, *The Problem of God* (Yale University 1964). p 70 (cf also Catechism par. 237)
6 cf Nicholas Lash, *Believing Three Ways in One God* (SCM 1992), pp. 44-45
7 Margaret Hebblethwaite, *Motherhood and God* (Chapman 1984), pp. 137-138
8 cf Robert Murray, *Symbols of the Church and Kingdom* (Cambridge 1975), pp. 312-320
9 cf Margaret Hebblethwaite, op. cit. pp. 124-139
10 D Bonhoeffer, *Letters and Papers from Prison* (SCM 1971), p. 360
11 J Moltmann, *The Crucified God* (SCM 1974), p. 222

FURTHER READING

Catechism of the Catholic Church: pars. 200-278
Lash, Nicholas, *Believing Three Ways in One God* (SCM 1992)
LaCugna, Catherine, *God for Us* (Harper Collins 1992)
Moltmann, Jurgen, *The Crucified God* (SCM 1974)
Taylor, John V, *The Christlike God* (SCM 1992)
O'Donnel, John, *The Mystery of the Triune God* (Sheed & Ward 1988)

CHAPTER THREE

CREATOR OF HEAVEN AND EARTH

INSIGHTS OF MODERN SCIENCE

The Moment of the Big Bang

'Where do we come from?' Since the beginning of time, people have told stories of how the world came to be; and today is no exception. Indeed, the sales of Stephen Hawking's *A Brief History of Time* bear witness to wide-spread fascination in our own time. His theory, accepted by many, is that fifteen billion years ago an immeasurably small and hot point of infinite density exploded into an unthinkable expansion of energy. Expansion and cooling continued and eventually the first generation of galaxies and stars was formed. Our own sun was formed about five billion years ago. Its energy, travelling at the speed of light, takes eight minutes to reach us, which puts it about ninety-three million miles away. The light of the next nearest star in our galaxy takes four years to reach us, and beyond that there are a further hundred thousand million such stars. So much for our own galaxy, which is only one of a hundred billion others that are visible to modern telescopes.

Unimaginable Unity in Diversity

It all staggers the imagination; everything that exists, in its infinite diversity, comes from one infinitesimal bit of matter. We are not equipped for coping with its incredible vastness and its aeons of time. But even within the scope of our own tiny planet, it is difficult to come to terms with the extent of diversity. Biologists have found in a single square foot of topsoil an inch deep 'an average of 1,356 living creatures'.[1] And with the advance in technology, we are able to experience such diversity in proportions and in detail unlike anything we have known before. Yet all has a common origin: 'We with all other living creatures have emerged in time out of the non-living world of water, air and rocks which seem so distinct and different from us.'[2] More than ever, we are able to appreciate the perspective of the Psalmist: 'I look up at your heavens, shaped by your fingers, at the moon and the stars you set firm – what are human beings that you spare a thought for them, or the child of Adam that you care for him?' (Psalm 8:3-4).

Fragile, Vulnerable and Precious

It is only within the last few decades that we have been able to view the earth from space. The picture is that of a brightly coloured planet revolving in a sea of black emptiness, a planet teeming with life in a galaxy that to our knowledge contains no other fertile planets. It is a most privileged view of the earth, so vulnerable and fragile, and yet so precious because, as far as we know, utterly unique. It brings home to us, as no other picture does, that we are all in this together, for there is no possibility of our being able to live elsewhere. It is our home and, therefore, it is vitally important that we take care of it.

Our planet is fragile, too, from another perspective. Scientists, like Bernard Lovell, tell us that if the universe had emerged a fraction of a second faster or slower it would all have collapsed back into itself. And again, if our planet had not come to rotate around the sun in nearly circular orbits, life could never have evolved because the extremes of temperature would have been too great. Indeed, at every critical moment in the long process of evolution, the margin for error was very slim. Just one degree either way and life could have been snuffed out as in the case of Mercury and Venus. And so everything is so finely balanced; all things are so mutually dependent upon each other from the beginning. Without plants, clean air, and water, we would quickly perish. We are citizens together on a planet that is our common home; and so, once again, we must recognise our responsibilities and take care of it. But do we?

A PLANET IN CRISIS

The Nuclear Threat

Nuclear extinction, although not quite so imminent as was felt just a few years ago, would mean the extinction of all life. It would be an appalling annihilation and one for which we would be directly responsible. Our planet, teeming with the rich diversity of life we have already referred to, would simply be wiped out. In the words of the American Bishops: 'Nuclear War represents a potentially catastrophic threat to the physical environment on which human life depends". The more one thinks about it, the more unthinkable it becomes.

Although the danger of such a war is not now so immediate, we must not underestimate the impact of conventional warfare. We need only recall the after-effects of the Gulf War and the continuing devastation of former Yugoslavia. Furthermore, billions of pounds are spent year by year on weapons of war which can only kill and destroy. In a world in which the rich continually get richer, where vast human resources in terms of skill and ingenuity are used in making weapons of destruction, we hear of millions of people suffering from malnutrition in countries where one child in five dies at or shortly after birth. The money required to provide adequate food, water, education, health, and housing for everyone in the world has been estimated at 12 billion pounds a year. It is a huge sum of money . . . about as much as the world spends on arms every two weeks!

Ecological Devastation

Unlike the nuclear threat, or even conventional warfare, ecological devastation is a gradual process which takes a little while for us to notice. Indeed, many of us can simply accept it as a natural concomitant of industrial progress. Furthermore, fewer and fewer people live on farms, close to nature, in the country, where we couldn't fail to notice the damage to the quality of life and even to the conditions necessary for life on earth. We need to realise that we live on a planet with limited resources that can be irretrievably lost. If we continue to poison our land, air and water, and waste our timber, mineral, and other natural resources, then we are heading for disaster for all forms of life on earth, including ourselves. Some predictions might sound alarmist, but there can be no doubt that considerable devastation is now taking place. The widespread use of chemicals has poisoned so much of the natural fertility of our soil; industrial pollution causes acid rain which has polluted thousands of freshwater lakes in Canada and Scandinavia and is destroying the Black Forest in Germany; and there is the release of billions of tons of carbon dioxide into the atmosphere which threatens the whole global climate of our planet.

In response to such a threat, arising both from the possibility of a nuclear holocaust and from continuing ecological devastation, we need to affirm with ever greater urgency our faith in God as Creator. Such faith can only possibly fill us with awe and overwhelming wonder, especially when we look upon our planet and the vast expanse of creation from the privileged position we hold today. It can only inspire us to recognise that we are all inhabitants of one common home for which we are only too pleased to take responsibility (cf Catechism par. 283).

'IN THE BEGINNING GOD CREATED THE HEAVENS AND THE EARTH'

(GENESIS 1:1)

Experience of God as Saviour

The Jewish people first learned of God from what they experienced in their own history. Around 1280BC, God engaged them in a relationship neither known nor experienced by any other people. They came to realise that they were related to God in a unique way. Indeed, they claimed to owe their existence as a people to a direct, creative act of God. Under the leadership of Moses, they made their escape from Egypt and crossed into Palestine – an event which became forever cherished in their memory as the Exodus. It was the moment they came into being as the People of God (Deuteronomy 26:5-10). Throughout their turbulent history they were always aware of their relationship to a single, powerful and living God. They were profoundly convinced that they had been specially chosen – a conviction sealed by a covenant. It was this covenant which bonded and held them together: 'For you are a people consecrated to Yahweh your God; of all the peoples on earth, you have been chosen by Yahweh your God to be his own people' (Deuteronomy 7:6). Apart from this covenant, they would be 'No-People', without hope and without life. Within the covenant, they came to know God as their God, slow to anger, abounding in steadfast love (Exodus 34:6), and utterly dependable (Isaiah 54:10). It was out of this experience that they came to recognise the hand of their God in the making of the world (cf Catechism pars. 287-288).

It is God Alone who Creates

Pagan creation stories present many gods and goddesses as creators. Faced with infinite variety and richness, violence and unpredictability, there seemed to be no alternative to accepting a whole pantheon of gods and goddesses who were caught up in the never-ending process of life and death, chaos and order. Such an understanding would seem to be the only alternative to a totally impersonal world, devoid of meaning.

Against all of this, a small nation proclaimed that there was only one God, supreme and unequalled, who was responsible for all that exists. Their world, too, gave evidence of disorder and chaos; they knew hunger and injustice, the failure of harvests, and the evil of warfare and incurable diseases. But they had come to place their trust in God who, having brought them out of the land of Egypt, would certainly be able to bring them out of all the chaos that surrounded them. 'Lift up your eyes and look: he who created these things leads out their army in order, summoning each of them by name. So mighty is his power, so great his strength that not one fails to answer' (Isaiah 40:26). And in Psalm 24:1-2: 'To Yahweh belong the earth and all it contains, the world and all who live there; it is he who laid its foundations on the seas, on the flowing waters fixed it firm.' And again in Isaiah: 'He who sits enthroned above the circle of the earth, the inhabitants of which are like grasshoppers, spreads out the heavens like a cloth, spreads them out like a tent to live in' (Isaiah 40:22).

It is this expression of faith which finds its classic expression in the opening chapters of Genesis. He is majestically alone and one, so that his word ('let there be light') is enough to bring things into being. The sun, moon and stars, the earth and all it contains are his creatures (cf Catechism pars. 289-290).

In God's Image

Man and woman stand at the apex of creation in the image and likeness of their maker (Genesis 1:26). This means that God has established men and women as his *representatives* on earth in a unique way and, as such, they are given a share in his sovereignty over all that he has made. This does not give us a licence to exploit it as we please. We are called to be responsible adults, the only species on the planet who really knows the creation story and so can take on the responsibility as partners for its well-being. This is brought out especially in the second account of creation (Genesis 2:7) where it is stressed that we come from the earth and are truly part of it. Men and women are created for the earth! Through the voices of men and women all creation can declare the greatness of God. Psalm 8 expresses the matter with great beauty: 'You have made him little less than a god, you have crowned him with glory and beauty, made him lord of the works of your hands, put all things under his feet, sheep and cattle all of them, and even the wild beasts, birds in the sky, fish in the sea, when he makes his way across the ocean. Yahweh, our Lord, how majestic your name throughout the world' (Psalm 8:5-9; cf Catechism pars. 356-361; 369-373).

And God Saw that it was Very Good

When we speak of God creating the world 'in the beginning', we are not suggesting that God is more present, more real, more active *then* than at any other point in time. Rather, we are speaking of that creative love of God which holds all things in being throughout the whole course of their evolution. Our God is equally present to every moment with the fullness of his love. A later generation was to describe this love as 'creating out of nothing' (2 Maccabees 7:28), which means that all is totally dependent on God and nothing can separate us from God. A passage from the Book of Wisdom expresses this point beautifully: 'Yes, you love everything that exists, and nothing that you have made disgusts you, since, if you had hated something, you would not have made it. And how could a thing subsist, had you not willed it? Or, how be preserved, if not called forth by you? No, you spare all, since all is yours, Lord, lover of life! For your imperishable spirit is in everything' (Wisdom 11:24-26).

After each act of creation God sees that what he has made is good, until finally we read: 'God saw all that he had made, and indeed it was very good' (Genesis 1:31). No matter how flawed the world may be, no matter how fragmented and broken, no matter how hostile or frightening, he who has made the world sees it and declares it to be good. This declaration is not made once and for all; rather, God constantly recognises the goodness of all that he has made. He blesses 'all creatures great and small' (v. 22), and he blesses the man and the woman (v. 28). All things have their being through the love of God who is their maker, lover, and keeper (cf Catechism pars. 309-314).

CREATED IN CHRIST

'Through Him all Things Came into Being' (John 1:3)

This faith of God in the goodness of all he created finds its fullest expression in the image of God we call Jesus Christ. His coming is a culmination of that process set in motion millions upon millions of years ago at the dawn of time. The declaration that all is good finds its fulfilment in those words spoken on the occasion of Jesus' baptism: 'You are my Son, the Beloved; my favour rests on you' (Mark 1:11). In Jesus, we know that, together with the whole of creation, we are absolutely cherished. There continues to be disorder and disharmony but the stance of Jesus is opposed to all forms of gloomy pessimism. Throughout his life, he proclaimed the truth of Genesis, asserting the essential goodness of all things. As one writer has described him: 'He was not just the man who healed lepers and made the blind to see. He was also the man who stilled the storm and walked on the water, whom the wild beasts did not harm; who often communed with nature, going up to the hills to pray or walking by the side of the lake. His parables were filled with images from the natural world – from mustard seeds and grains of sand to vineyards and fields of wheat.'[4] Jesus was utterly at home in our world and totally in harmony with nature.

It is no wonder that on a number of occasions in the New Testament Jesus is set firmly within the framework of God's creative love: 'Yet for us there is only one God, the Father from whom all things come and for whom we exist, and one Lord Jesus Christ, through whom all things come and through whom we exist' (1 Corinthians 8:6). And again: 'He is the image of the unseen God . . . for in him were created all things . . . he exists before all things and in him all things hold together' (Colossians 1:15-18). And finally, from the Prologue of the Gospel according to St John: 'In the beginning was the Word .... He was with God in the beginning. Through him all things came into being, not one thing came into being except through him' (John 1:1-4).

'He Emptied Himself' *(Philippians 2:6)*

These words from St Paul's letter to the Philippians impress upon us that God's act of creation through his Son Jesus Christ is not without cost. Although it seems that God makes the world quite effortlessly by his word, that Word, St John tells us, is none other than the Word made flesh who, says St Paul 'emptied himself, taking the form of a slave . . . accepting death, death on a cross' (Philippians 2:6-8). From the very first moment, God has continually 'emptied himself', bestowing his limitless love upon every aspect of his creation, never once lapsing into indifference: 'He does not grow tired or weary, his understanding is beyond fathoming' (Isaiah 40:28). He takes delight in every detail of the universe from within: 'Mister God can love you right inside'.[5] To every detail he gives the closest attention, bringing it into being for its own sake, every detail worthy of reverence and respect. Such attention is reflected in the admirable attitude of Meister Eckhart: 'If I spent enough time with the tiniest creature – even a caterpillar – I would never have to prepare a sermon. So full of God is every creature.'[6]

The story of creation, therefore, can hardly be described simply as 'a marvellous celebratory event'. It has also been a story of struggle, destruction, waste, death and pain, and has inevitably affected the very heart of God. In the words of St Paul: 'We are well aware that the whole of creation, until this time, has been groaning in labour pains . . .' (Romans 8:22). In all our afflictions God is afflicted, and feels more keenly than we ever can every agony along the way. But, though 'mountains may go away and the hills may totter, my faithful love will never leave you, my covenant of peace will never totter' (Isaiah 54:10). And so, in the course of time, the endlessly generous fidelity of God is made known in Jesus, the Beloved, who through his passion and death, loves to the end. The cross is the sign of God's intimate involvement with us to the point of death and beyond.

VOICES OF TRADITION

A Long-Standing Counter-Witness

• *Focus on personal salvation*

Despite the overwhelming testimony of the scriptures concerning the full extent of God's love embracing the whole of creation, much of Western tradition has been preoccupied with the personal salvation of humankind. Such a concentration on the human condition has inevitably relegated all that is non-human to the periphery. The mighty acts of God are seen almost exclusively in the exodus of the Israelites from Egypt to the Promised Land and in the death and resurrection of Jesus; not upon the great explosion of creative energy that sustains the whole universe in being. It has been assumed that only in these moments do we come to know the name of God, in a manner that is not possible elsewhere. God's presence in creation came to be viewed simply as a backdrop to the real drama between God and sinners and their concern for salvation. The life of faith became increasingly separated from the celebration of the presence of God in nature.

• *Creation in the service of humanity*

Accompanying this preoccupation with personal salvation has been a very 'human-centred' view of creation. It was assumed that the only value the natural world possessed was to help people to salvation. Human beings held centre stage; all else was mere 'background'. A good example of this tendency is to be found in the writings of St Ignatius of Loyola.

> 'Man is created to praise, reverence and serve God, and by this means to save his soul. The other things on the face of the earth are created for man to help him in attaining the end for which he was created. Hence man is to make use of them in as far as they help him in the attainment

of his end, and he must rid himself of them in as
far as they prove a hindrance to him.'

There is no hint here of the goodness of creation in itself, so
strongly emphasised in the Scriptures. Indeed, some would
argue that St Ignatius' understanding of creation, shared by
so many others, has prepared the ground for a technology
which is increasingly destroying our planet.[7] Fortunately,
there have been other voices within Christian tradition, which
have been faithful to the vision of Genesis, the Psalms, and
indeed, Jesus himself.

Prophets of Creation

• Hildegard of Bingen (1098-1178)

Hildegard became a Benedictine nun at the age of fifteen and
led an uneventful life within her community until her visions
and revelations began in 1132. After centuries of neglect, she
is now recognised to be one of the most remarkable and
versatile women of the middle ages. She wrote poems, hymns,
and a morality play, besides works of medicine and natural
history. But it is her appreciation of the goodness of the
natural world which makes her especially important for us
today. In the following poem she delights in the love of the
Creator for his creation: 'I compare the great love of Creator
and creation to the same love and fidelity with which God
binds man and woman together. This is so that together they
might be creatively fruitful.' There is no ambiguity towards
creation in Hildegard. All living creatures emerge from God
as sparks: 'All the living sparks are rays of his splendour, just
as the rays of the sun proceed from the sun itself. And how
would God be known to be life except through the living
things which glorify him?'[8]

• St Francis of Assisi (1182-1226)

Of all the prophets who have proclaimed the wonders of our
world, St Francis of Assisi must be the most well-known.
Towards the end of his life, when blind and in great pain, he

wrote one of the greatest of all Christian hymns, the *Canticle of the Sun*. The created world and everything within it constantly reminded St Francis of the grandeur and wonder of God himself: the rocks reminded him of that 'rock which was Christ'; the lambs of the field symbolised the Lamb of God, trees were symbols of the cross, and lights represented the Light of the World. Everything in the natural world led Francis' mind and heart to God.

• *Teilhard de Chardin (1881-1955)*

Nearer to our own time, these same insights have found expression in the writings of Teilhard de Chardin. He entered the Society of Jesus in 1899 but very soon he came into conflict with the Church because of his writings. His religious superiors were alarmed by his optimistic view of the evolving universe and barred him from teaching. In 1951, he was exiled from Europe to spend the rest of his days in New York until he died in 1955. In 1957 a decree of the Holy Office (now Congregation for the Doctrine of Faith) required his books to be removed from libraries, and forbade their sale in Catholic bookshops and their translation into other languages. Soon after his death, however, his many books were published and have since become extremely popular, especially *Divine Milieu* and *Hymn of the Universe*. The following passage is not untypical of his writings:

> 'Blessed be you, perilous matter, violent sea, untameable passion. Blessed be you, mighty matter, irresistible march of evolution, reality ever new born. Blessed be you, universal matter, immeasurable time, boundless ether, you who by overflowing and dissolving our narrow standards of measurement reveal to us the dimensions of God. I acclaim you as the divine milieu, charged with creative power, as the ocean stirred by the Spirit, as the clay moulded and infused with life by the incarnate Word.'[9]

IMPLICATIONS OF FAITH IN GOD'S CREATION

Priests of Creation

As we have seen, men and women have been given a unique role in the working out of God's plan for the whole of creation. We alone, amongst all the creatures of God, are made in his image and likeness. We alone are able to be conscious observers of the purpose of creation and so are commissioned by God to be responsible partners for its well-being. We are called to share in God's delight of his creation for its own sake; to develop a natural curiosity into the wonders of creation; and to express compassionate care for the environment in which we live. More than that, we are called upon to voice the prayers and express the thanksgivings not just of ourselves but of the whole of creation. This is what it means to be priests of creation – providing a channel through which our fellow creatures have access to eternity.

Celebrating the Sacraments

It is only within such a view of the world that we are able to appreciate the sacraments of Christian faith. By making use of the simple things of this earth – water, bread, wine and oil, – we are enabled to see with fresh eyes the full richness of our dignity as human beings and our responsibility for the created world in which we live. And so, the water of Baptism must challenge us to maintain the purity of our natural water systems – rain, running streams, lakes and oceans. They must be fresh, clean and life-giving, if water is to continue to be an effective symbol for the new life that comes to us through the death and resurrection of Jesus. Similarly, when celebrating the Eucharist, sharing food and drink in memory of Jesus, we cannot be indifferent to so many millions of people who constantly live with hunger, many of them dying of malnutrition. We cannot celebrate the presence of the Bread of Life without being challenged to do something about this appalling reality. We cannot receive the bread of life without sharing it with those in need. Indeed, we must become the bread of life for others.

Practical Suggestions

In addition to our celebration of the sacraments, the annual Harvest Festival provides us with an opportunity for celebrating the gift of the natural world. Both Christian Aid and CAFOD are now producing valuable material making us conscious of the needs of the environment and of the growing gap between the rich and the poor. It would seem that we have a lot to learn from young children on these occasions. They intuitively recognise themselves as part of creation and not above it, especially in their solidarity with other creatures. And so, for instance, they often possess wide powers of sympathy for injured animals, demonstrating such a marvellous natural affection that we need to encourage.[10]

There is room, too, for a Spring Service which might explore the themes of growth and rebirth, focussing especially on the goodness of God's creation. There is so much in the world which speaks of struggle, destruction, waste, death and pain. But, no matter how flawed the world may be, no matter how fragmented and broken, no matter how hostile or frightening, we need to express our faith in the goodness of all that God has made. We are called to be a people of hope: a people always ready to heal, to rebuild, to restore and replant; a people always believing in the possibilities of God. A Spring Service would be an appropriate way of celebrating such a faith.[11]

And finally, there needs to be a raising of consciousness about the responsible use of limited resources. All too often we live under the illusion that there is plenty of water, plenty of oil, plenty of whatever we need and want. In fact, there is not. Another illusion is that my small demand on the world's resources cannot make much difference and does not really matter. In fact, it matters a lot. We must overcome these temptations and recognise that a responsible use of resources

is vital for the future of our planet. This may mean only using
material that can be recycled, changing our eating habits to
food that is home-grown and more healthy, conserving energy
wherever possible, and being encouraged to walk, cycle or use
public transport. In so many ways, we can express in simple
practical ways the responsibility that belongs to each of us as
stewards of God's creation.[12]

NOTES

1 Sallie McFague, *The Body of God* (SCM 1993), p. 38; for what follows
   cf pp38-63
2 John V Taylor, *The Christlike God* (SCM 1992). p. 184
3 cited by Sean McDonagh, *To Care for the Earth* (Chapman 1986), p. 192
4 Ian Bradley, *God is Green* (DLT 1990), pp. 78ff
5 Fynn, *Mister God, This is Anna* (Fountain 1974), p. 41
6 cf Sean McDonagh, op cit. p. 46
7 cited by Angela Tilby, *Science and the Soul* (SPCK 1992), p. 220
8 Bowie and Davies, *Hildegard of Bingen, an anthology* (SPCK 1992), p. 28
9 Teilhard de Chardin, *Hymn of the Universe* (Fontana 1960), p. 63
10 cf Edward Echlin, *Four Useful Guidelines to assist a Greener Church*
   in Catholic Gazette, (July 1991)
11 Ian Bradley, God is Green (DLT 1990), pp. 107-113
12 Edward Echlin, art. cit. pp. 17-18; cf also Sallie McFague, op. cit. p.121

FURTHER READING

Catechism of the Catholic Church: pars. 279-379
Bowie/Davies, *Hildegarde of Bingen: an Anthology* (SPCK 1992)
Bradley, Ian, *God is Green* (DLT 1990)
McDade, John (ed) *Creation*, The Month, November 1990
McDonagh, Sean, *To Care for the Earth* (Chapman 1986)
McFague, Sallie, *The Body of God* (SCM 1993)
Sachs, John R, *The Christian Vision of Humanity* (Liturgical Press 1991)
Taylor, John V, *The Christlike God* (SCM 1992)
Tilby, Angela, *Science and the Soul* (SPCK 1992)

CHAPTER FOUR

JESUS CHRIST: HIS ONLY SON, OUR LORD

IMPACT OF JESUS IN THE FLESH

Experience of Jesus as Lord

One of the distinctive features of the lives of many Christians today is the experience of Jesus as Lord; he is alive and real in a way they have never felt before. This experience stands in marked contrast to a tradition within the Church which has insisted for more than four centuries that we could not have a direct knowledge of the state of grace. Grace, we were told, belongs to a realm utterly beyond human consciousness. We knew about grace and its vital importance for heaven not from personal experience but simply from being told so by the teaching authority of the Church.

In recent times, however, strong voices are being raised within the Christian Churches testifying to their experience of Jesus as Lord. They come principally from charismatic communities who point to the truth of the promises of Jesus: a peace which this world cannot give (John 14:27); a joy that no one can take away (John 16:22); rest and refreshment to those overburdened (Matthew 11:28-30); a life that can only be described in terms of being born again (John 3:3), regenerated and renewed (Titus 3:5), and changed into new creatures (2 Corinthians 5:17). These words can only possibly have meaning if their truth is felt at the level of human experience.

This experience represents nothing less than a recovery, in varying degrees, of that transformation that overcame the first disciples of Jesus. We need only recall the experience of the two disciples on the road to Emmaus. As they walked in sadness away from Jerusalem, the mysterious stranger drew near to them and walked along with them, unfolding for them in a wonderful way the meaning of the Scriptures. Reflecting later upon their experience, they said to one another: 'Did not our hearts burn within us as he talked to us on the road and explained the scriptures to us?' (Luke 24:32). They came to know as they had never done before the personal presence of God in the Spirit of Jesus Christ.

Such is the experience of increasing numbers of Christians in our own time: if Jesus is for real then his presence must be felt in the depths of our being here and now. In the words of St Paul: 'It is not I that live but Christ that lives in me' (Galatians 2:20).

The Word Became Flesh

Because of our renewed faith in the Word that was made flesh, the Christian Churches are speaking much more positively of the richness of human beings, of the personal dignity that belongs to each of us, of the goodness of the world in which we live. To know that this was not always the case, we need only remind ourselves of the catechism question: 'Of which must I take most care, my body or my soul?' And the answer seemed all too obvious: 'My soul'.

Traditional Christianity has encouraged in this way an ingrained suspicion of the flesh, of sexuality, and of the world in general. The soul was regarded as the seat of thought and personality; the body was considered as an outer garment which weighed the soul down, a prison which chained the soul to earth, a strait-jacket which restricted the soul's freedom. Death appeared as the soul's friend and the body's enemy. Such a bias against the body and sexuality has encouraged within people a very poor image of themselves. It has convinced people of their own sinfulness; it has created a perpetual state of guilt, of fear, of worthlessness, of hopelessness, with little experience of forgiveness and that sense of being accepted.

Today, the tide is turning. We are beginning to speak, once again, of the full richness of human beings and the created world in which we live. We cannot turn our back on a world that has been created out of the love of God and constantly proclaims his glory, a world in which Jesus has made his home. We cannot turn our back upon sexuality and the body when all experience tells us that we can only exist, live, love, share, understand, communicate in the body. We live bodily, both in this world and in eternity, or we do not live at all. That is why Jesus became one with us in the flesh; it is the only way in which he could speak to us of the love of God (cf Catechism pars. 363-367).

Jesus: Liberator of the Poor

Reflecting upon the historical life of Jesus has made us appreciate the social implications of our Christian commitment. We cannot be true disciples of Jesus Christ and at the same time be indifferent to the needs of the world in which we live. And yet, here too, we have suffered from what can only be described as a terrible blindness. A negative view of the world, of sexuality, of the flesh, has encouraged a withdrawal from the world, a spirit of non-involvement in the social and political problems of the time. Real spirituality, it has been said, demands that the church keep out of politics, concentrate its attention on religious matters, and not be concerned with social structures and their impact on people's lives.

This outlook was further intensified by the traditional preoccupation with the next life which thereby seemed to devalue the present one. If our real treasure is in another world, then it is not too difficult to become indifferent to the injustices of this world. We cannot deny that there has been justification for Karl Marx to identify religion as the opium of the people, exhorting the oppressed and deprived to suffer patiently and willingly in the name of Jesus, expecting their reward for this beyond death.

Once again, many voices, especially in Latin America, are calling for a radical change of heart: without the preaching of justice there is no Gospel of Jesus Christ. At all times, the task of the church is to protest against injustice, to challenge what is inhuman, and to side with the poor and the oppressed. The church of Christ must continue the mission of Jesus: 'The spirit of the Lord is on me, for he has anointed me to bring the good news to the afflicted. He has sent me to proclaim liberty to captives, sight to the blind, to let the oppressed go free, to proclaim a year of favour from the Lord' (Luke 4:18).

Focus Upon the Historical Jesus

The inspiration for all these developments has come from a re-discovery of the historical Jesus. Practically all Christian theologians are agreed upon the need to make one's starting-point the utter reality of the manhood of Jesus if we are to grasp the challenge of his impact upon us. In the words of Karl Rahner: 'We must regard as heretical any understanding of the incarnation which makes the humanity of Jesus only a disguise used by God to signal his challenging presence . . . It is only when one sees Jesus as fully and unequivocally human that his lordship and divinity appears for the staggering mystery that it is.'[1] To appreciate the reasons for this emphasis today, it is important that we take a brief look at the historical development of the church's understanding of Jesus.

HISTORICAL SKETCH

(CF CATECHISM PARS. 464-469)

Arius v. Nicaea (c. 325)

• *The position of Arius*

Arius, a priest of Alexandria at the beginning of the fourth century, was the first to state the problem of Jesus with precision. His starting-point was his affirmation of the absolute uniqueness and transcendence of God: 'We acknowledge one God, who is alone eternal, alone without beginning, alone possessing immortality.' The being of God, therefore, cannot be shared or communicated. For God to impart his being to another would imply that he is subject to change, which is inconceivable. Jesus Christ, therefore, cannot be the true Son of God; the most that can be said of him is that 'he comes from the Father as the most perfect creature'. He appealed to the Scriptures: Jesus grew in wisdom (Luke 2:52); he did not know the time of the Second Coming (Mark 13:32); he experienced anguish of heart (Mark 14:34), felt abandoned by the Father (Mark 15:34), suffered and died. These scriptural texts, concluded Arius, excluded the claim that Jesus was the Son of God. [2]

• *The reply of Nicaea*

The Arian question received its definitive answer at the Council of Nicaea (now Iznic in Modern Turkey) in 325: 'We believe in one Lord Jesus Christ . . . begotten out of the Father . . . God from God, light from light, true God from true God, begotten not made, one in substance with the Father.' The intention of the Fathers at Nicaea was simply to state the sense of the Scriptures against the distortion of Arius. They wanted to emphasise that, no matter how much God is to be thought of as transcending our world, he is, nevertheless, to be thought of as involved in, concerned with, and active in our world, especially in the life and ministry of Jesus Christ. In Jesus we have to do with nothing less than God himself. It is only on the basis of such faith that Jesus can be acknowledged as our Saviour.

• *The impact of Nicaea*

This reply of Nicaea to Arius made a tremendous impact on the life of the Church and to a great extent it explains the prevailing emphases today. Such stress was placed upon the divinity of Christ that very often mere lip-service was given to the fact of his humanity. One noted liturgist has shown how this emphasis has been reflected in our devotion to the Eucharist. [3] From the fourth century, there began a serious decline in the numbers of people going to communion so that, during the Middle Ages, the Fourth Lateran Council had to insist that people went to communion at least once a year at Easter time (more popularly known as Easter duties). The shape of eucharistic devotion had changed from receiving the Eucharist as daily food to the adoration of Christ in the Blessed Sacrament. To understand a little better the impact of Nicaea, we need to examine two basic approaches to Christ which emerged at that time.

Alexandria v. Antioch

Though the church as a whole has always acknowledged Jesus as fully God and fully human, there have generally been two schools of thought: one lays stress on the divinity of Christ; the other places emphasis upon the humanity of Christ. The Alexandrians started from the divinity of Christ, and in their zeal for this truth tended to minimise Christ's humanity. The Antiochenes, on the other hand, were anxious to stress the reality of Christ's human nature and so tended to pass over his divinity. Establishing the right balance proved to be very difficult.

• *The Antiochene School*

To the Antiochenes, the less guarded statements of the Alexandrians seemed to suggest that the humanity of Jesus was a mere illusion. Examples of such statements would be as follows: 'It would be ridiculous to imagine that the body of Jesus, in order to exist, had the usual human needs. He only took food and ate in order that we should not teach about him in a docetic manner, whereby he only seemed to be human' (Clement of Alexandria); 'the natural condition of Christ's body and soul was complete freedom from the usual human needs: the miracle was that he did feel weary' (St Hilary); 'He permitted his own flesh to weep a little, although it was in its nature tearless and incapable of grief' (Cyril of Alexandria). The Antiochenes rightly protested against such teaching because it did not respect the genuine humanity of Jesus as he is portrayed in the Gospels. They argued that, if the humanity of Jesus is neglected or minimised, the relevance of what God has accomplished in Jesus Christ is certainly to be neglected or minimised as well. In the terse comment of Gregory of Nazianzen: 'What God has not assumed, that he has not redeemed'.

• *The Alexandrian School*

The Alexandrians, on the other hand, thought that the Antiochenes were people who said that Jesus was merely a good man who was 'adopted' by God as his Son. Here, too, it must be said that there was considerable justification. In their concern to establish the genuinely human character of the figure of Christ (like Arius), they found it difficult to do justice to the identity of Jesus Christ as the Son of God. The Alexandrians rightly objected that if the living God is not personally involved in the life of Jesus then we are still in our sins. Their point of view was canonised by the Council of Ephesus (431) when it declared: 'One and the same is the eternal Son of the Father and the Son of the Virgin Mary, born of time after the flesh; therefore, she may rightly be called "Mother of God".'

Council of Chalcedon (451)

This debate concerning the person of Jesus Christ, sometimes involving bitter discussion, culminated in 451 in the definition of the Council of Chalcedon. 'We confess one and the same Son, our Lord Jesus Christ, perfect in Godhead, perfect in manhood, truly God and truly man . . .' The declared intent of the Fathers of Chalcedon was to exhort and to encourage all Christians to join together in peace and harmony amongst themselves in their confession of faith in Christ. They recognised the positive aspects of both the Alexandrians' and Antiochenes' point of view and affirmed that equal emphasis must be placed upon the divine and the human in Jesus Christ. On the one hand, the radical transformation of human possibilities in our world can only come about by an action of God in and through the power of the risen Jesus. On the other hand, the Jesus in whom we place our unconditional trust, and in whom we encounter the divine face to face, is the Jesus of history, one who lived his life in the same human situation as ourselves, and with whom there can be genuine solidarity.

In the words of Chalcedon, therefore, Jesus Christ is totally divine and totally human. To place emphasis upon one aspect at the expense of the other is simply to misunderstand the mystery of the incarnation. There cannot be any conflict between God and humankind; on the contrary, the closer we are to God the more human we become and this is fully exemplified in the life of Jesus Christ.

Unfortunately, so much of Christian tradition has tended to view all emphases upon the humanity of Christ as a threat to the dimension of the divine. This is simply a reflection of our general tendency to defend the sovereignty of God by denigrating the possibilities of men and women, by having such a negative attitude towards the body, sexuality, and the world in which we live. Such a view is totally incompatible with the Gospel. The Word became flesh; our God reveals himself as invitation, not threat; He is not jealous of human greatness but rather is revealed in human greatness. This is surely the heart of the Gospel and the fundamental significance of Jesus – here, above all, is expressed the glory of God in a living person. It is this basic correspondence between the divine and the human that modern approaches to Christ wish to respect, and in doing so make their starting-point the humanity of Christ.

THE WORD BECAME FLESH

The Human Face of God

One writer has stated well the importance of this starting-point for an understanding of Christ: 'It is precisely in a human situation, and not in some imagined ideal situation, that we are found of God and hence are enabled to find him . . . What Christ accomplished is not above our heads, far off in the skies; it is here on this common earth, in simple human terms, in the sheer flesh and blood of our humanity.'[4] In other words, Jesus reveals God to us by being human and not in spite of being human. The humanity of Jesus does not hide God; on the contrary, it reveals him.

• *Jesus was born a Jew*

The first point we must make is that Jesus was born of Jewish parents and came from a long Jewish ancestry (cf Matthew 1:1-17). What he taught, how he looked at the world, his relationship to God as Father, is all set in the context of the Judaism of his age. In particular, from the tradition of Israel, he made his own the spirituality of the 'anawim', the poor in spirit or simple people, who placed all their trust in God, a spirituality so characteristic of his own mother, Mary: 'I am the handmaid of the Lord, let what you have said be done to me' (Luke 1:18). Indeed, to speak of Jesus as 'the Christ', God's anointed, sets him firmly within the whole history of Jewish expectation, with its memories, its psalms, and its prophetic writings. To accept the whole Christ must imply that we take hold of these memories and, especially, the psalms, and make them the substance of our prayer (Catechism par. 527).

• *The hidden life of Jesus*

Following the presentation of Jesus in the Temple, Luke comments that 'as the child grew to maturity, he was filled with wisdom; and God's favour was with him' (Luke 2:40). This same comment is repeated when Jesus returns home after being found amongst the teachers in the Temple: 'And Jesus increased in wisdom, in stature, and in favour with God and with people' (Luke 2:52). In the small town of Nazareth, Jesus experienced a normal family life until the time came for the beginning of his public ministry at the age of 30 or so. That nothing out of the ordinary happened during this time is reflected in the reaction of his neighbours when he later returned to his home town of Nazareth: 'Where did the man get this wisdom and these miraculous powers? This is the carpenter's son, surely? Is not his mother the woman called Mary, and his brothers James and Joseph and Simon and Jude? His sisters, too, are they not all here with us? So where did the man get it all?' (Matthew 13:54-57). This comment, perhaps more than any other, reflects the extent to which Jesus became one with us and made his home amongst us. He lived inconspicuously amongst his neighbours, slowly and patiently growing towards that maturity which would prepare him for his 'hour'. It was a time for silence, quietly absorbing all that human experience had to offer before embarking on his public ministry (cf Catechism pars. 531-533).

• *At home in our world*

Because Jesus was our brother according to the flesh and felt so much at home in our world, he had an intimate appreciation of the beauty of creation. His vision and imagination are expressed with such warmth and spontaneity in that most famous and lyrical of all passages in the Gospel – the sermon on the birds of the air and the lilies of the field (Matthew 6:25-34). It is a picture trembling with life: 'Look at the birds in the sky. They do not sow or reap . . . Think of the flowers growing in the fields; they never have to work or spin . . .'. Jesus wants us to wear the smile of those flowers, bear the carefree attitude of the birds, so that all may come to associate godliness with life and freedom. Jesus, too, is at home with all kinds of people. He dined with people of respectable standing, like the Pharisees; he mixed with tax-collectors and sinners, who were regarded as social outcasts; and he spoke to them all with great compassion and understanding. His impact upon Zacchaeus, for example, was typical: a tax-collector, a hated man of society, as a result of meeting Jesus, is totally transformed because he felt accepted, with his personal dignity restored.

• *'Tempted in every way that we are'*

What explains the impact of Jesus is nothing less than his sheer humanity; he presents himself as one who understands the weakness of the human condition from personal experience. A most dramatic scriptural text in this respect comes from the Letter to the Hebrews: 'For the high priest we have is not incapable of feeling our weaknesses with us, but has been put to the test in exactly the same way as ourselves, apart from sin . . . he can sympathise with those who are ignorant or who have gone astray because he too is subject to the limitations of weakness' (Hebrews 4:15; 5:1). Because of his experience of human weakness, Jesus is able to reach out to every kind of human suffering. He gradually enters into those domains of injustice, oppression and evil, in which the compassion of God is most needed. In his moment of darkness, naked and crucified upon the cross, Jesus embraces all men and women, sharing with them that sense of abandonment, the terrible fear that their lives are without meaning. He enters into their situation of suffering all the way to the bitter end and, in the words of Teresa of Avila, becomes an ever present and most extraordinary companion and friend (Catechism pars. 538-540).

• *Was Jesus able to sin?*

Though Jesus was tempted in every way that we are, the author of Hebrews affirms that Jesus was without sin. Does this mean that Jesus, although tempted, could not sin, or does it mean that Jesus could sin but, in fact, did not sin? For, if Jesus could not possibly sin, then he would not be really human like us. A few reflections are in order here.

First of all, it is impossible to verify historically whether Jesus sinned or not. It is only through faith in the resurrection of Jesus that we are able to affirm that Jesus is the only-begotten Son of God and therefore, in retrospect, could not have sinned.

Secondly, throughout his life, he lived in the company of sinners and was more than willing to be taken for a sinner.

And thirdly, when we consider Jesus before his resurrection, as a man of faith on the way, we can say that Jesus had the capacity to sin but in fact did not sin. The author to the Hebrews speaks of Jesus as the 'perfected man who became the source of eternal salvation' (Hebrews 5:7). Throughout his life, he continued to choose the Father's will and so it became increasingly impossible morally for Jesus to sin. There lies his uniqueness and greatness. [5]

The Divine Face of Humanity

• 'God with us'

As we reflect on the human experience of Jesus, we affirm in faith that in Jesus we have to do with nothing less than God himself. Throughout the pages of the Old Testament, there was tremendous stress upon the transcendence of God, whom 'the heavens and their own heavens cannot contain' (2 Chronicles 6:18). Nevertheless, there was a growing appreciation of a God who has come close to the people he loves: 'What great nation has its gods as near as Yahweh our God is to us whenever we call to him?' (Deuteronomy 4:7). Yet even such an experience pales into insignificance when we reflect upon the closeness of God in the person of Jesus Christ. The God who remains beyond all human knowing and beyond all human discourse, has clothed himself in human nature and so made it possible for us to speak of him, to reach out and touch him. St Matthew calls Jesus 'Emmanuel, which means God with us'. (Matthew 1:25), while St John expresses it more dramatically: 'The Word became flesh and dwelt amongst us' (John 1:14). Here lies the uniqueness of the human life of Jesus: it speaks in language that we can understand of a heart shaped by immeasurable love – the inner heart of God passionately concerned for his people. In the words of St Paul's letter to the Colossians: 'He is the image of the unseen God' (Colossians 1:15-16). And in St John's Gospel: 'He who has seen me has seen the Father'. (John 14:9).

• *The virginal conception of Jesus*

Such belief in the divinity of Jesus would not be affected if Jesus had been the child of a normal human marriage. Nevertheless, until the eighteenth century, Christianity was unanimous in its conviction that Jesus was conceived of the virgin Mary, without the involvement of a human father. This was taken to be the unambiguous meaning of the infancy narratives in Matthew and Luke. And so, in the words of St Ignatius at the beginning of the second century:

> 'You are firmly convinced about our Lord, who is truly of the race of David according to the flesh, Son of God according to the will and power of God, truly born of a virgin . . . he was truly nailed to the tree for us in his flesh under Pontius Pilate . . . he truly suffered, as he is also truly risen.'
> (Ad Smyrn. 1-2, cited by Catechism par. 496; cf also pars. 496-507.)

In recent times, however, a number of objections to the doctrine of the virginal conception have been raised: it would seem to separate him from the rest of the human race and thereby make him irrelevant to the human quest for salvation; it seems to suggest that it would be demeaning for Jesus to come in to the world through the sexual love of a man and woman; and finally, what is said of Jesus, surely, applies to the whole Christian community, 'born not of blood, nor of the will of the flesh nor of the will of man, but of God' (John 1:12-13).

In all of this we need to remember that Mary's biological virginity, although important, is a secondary issue. Whilst historical evidence cannot prove it one way or the other, we accept it as a tangible sign that the birth of Jesus is entirely due to an act of God. Although the faith of Mary and the single-mindedness of her obedience to God play a vital role, it is God's initiative for the sake of the world that is utterly fundamental. The virginal conception of Jesus speaks of the divine origin of our saviour, who is none other than 'God with us'.

• *Jesus' relationship to the Father*

Jesus' consciousness of his unique relationship to the Father was the real driving force of his whole mission and ministry. This would have been shaped, first of all, by his Jewish background and his acute sensitivity to the closeness of God to his people (Deuteronomy 4:7; Deuteronomy 32:6; Hosea 11:1). Another factor would, undoubtedly, have been his parents, Mary and Joseph, and the special circumstances surrounding his birth, brought about by a special act of God. During the 'hidden years' spent in Nazareth, Jesus' experience of family, his experience of prayer, and his attendance at the synagogue, would all have served to shape his understanding of God as 'Abba'. The use of this term undoubtedly goes back to Jesus himself. In Mark 14:36, for example, Jesus prays: 'Abba, Father! For you everything is possible. Take this cup away from me. But let it be as you, not I, would have it.' Such a way of praying would have been quite unthinkable to a Jew. The term 'Abba' expresses familiarity and intimacy and that Jesus should dare to address God in such a familiar way came as a shock. Furthermore, Jesus always prays to God as 'my Father' and is careful to distinguish between 'my Father' and 'your Father'. His greatest gift to us is contained in the invitation to pray: 'Our Father'.

• *Jesus and the kingdom of God*

This unique relationship that Jesus experienced with God as Father enabled him to speak with authority on the kingdom of God. He begins his public ministry by proclaiming: '. . . the time is fulfilled, and the kingdom of God is at hand; repent and believe in the Gospel' (Mark 1:14-15). And again, after reading the Book of Isaiah, he says: 'Today this scripture has been fulfilled in your hearing' (Luke 4:21). It is quite obvious that Jesus is aware that the kingdom of God comes about in and through his own person. And the signs that accompany it are those Jesus gives to John the Baptist: 'The blind see again, and the lame walk, those suffering from virulent skin-diseases are cleansed, and the deaf hear, the dead are raised to life and the good news is proclaimed to the poor' (Matthew 11:4). Indeed, all the words and deeds of Jesus are about the significance of the kingdom of God that is close at hand. He speaks with authority on the kind of values that must characterise the kingdom: 'You have learnt how it was said . . . but I say to you . . . ' In asking his disciples to love their enemies he is lifting all limitations to love. This prescription Jesus himself put into practice throughout his life but, in a special way, during the meals that he shared with tax-collectors and sinners. When asked why he did this, he replied: 'It is not the healthy who need the doctor but the sick . . . I did not come to call the virtuous but sinners' (Matthew 9:12-13). Such meals symbolised the compassion, the risking, the reaching out, the total caring that so marked the life of Jesus (Catechism pars. 541-550).

It is through his death and resurrection, however, that Jesus is able to enter into our inmost being, fill us with his peace, unite us ever more closely to his own life, and become personally present to us in a way that was not possible during the days of his flesh. In the words of St Paul: 'I have been crucified with Christ, and I live now not with my own life but with the life of Christ who lives in me' (Galatians 2:20). Such is our union with Christ that the only way in which we can be with him is by being with those whom God has chosen as his own, especially the poor and the sick. Is it not upon recognition of this fact that our final judgement is based? 'I tell you solemnly, in so far as you did this to one of the least of these brothers of mine, you did it to me' (Matthew 25:40; cf Catechism pars. 426-429).

Notes

1 Karl Rahner, *Theological Investigations, vol. 4* (DLT 1966), pp. 117-118
2 J N D Kelly, *Early Christian Doctrines* (A & C Black 1965), pp. 226ff
3 J Jungmann, *The Mass of the Roman Rite* (London 1961), p. 62
4 N Pittenger, *Christology Reconsidered* (SCM 1970), pp. 39-40
5 B McDermott, *Word Become Flesh* (Liturgical Press, 1993) pp. 206-207

Further Reading

Cathechism of the Catholic Church: pars. 422-559
Kelly, J N D, *Early Christian Doctrines* (A & C Black 1965)
Lash, Nicholas, *Believing Three Ways in One God* (SCM 1992)
Lyons, Enda, *Jesus: Self-Portrait by God* (Columba 1994)
McDermott Brian, *Word Become Flesh* (Liturgical Press 1993)
Macquarrie John, *Jesus Christ in Modern Thought* (SCM 1990)
O'Collins Gerald, *Interpreting Jesus* (Chapman 1983)

CHAPTER FIVE

HE WAS CRUCIFIED, DIED, AND ROSE AGAIN

FOR US AND FOR OUR SALVATION

In the Nicene Creed which we recite each Sunday, we proclaim: 'For us (men) and for our salvation he came down from heaven.' In the Apostles' Creed, on the other hand, there is no mention of why Jesus died; it simply states that Jesus 'suffered under Pontius Pilate, was crucified, died, and was buried'. Nevertheless, it is important that we ask ourselves why it is that Jesus died for us and, indeed, why it is that God became human. This question belongs to a centuries old debate, reflected in the writings of St Thomas Aquinas – a Dominican (1228-1274) and John Duns Scotus – a Franciscan (1266-1308): if Adam had not sinned, would Christ have come?

St Thomas Aquinas argued that Christ only came amongst us because Adam sinned. It is only in response to our sinfulness that we come to know the love of God in the death and resurrection of Jesus. We know Jesus, therefore, above all as our redeemer and our response to him can only be one of gratitude. It is because of St Thomas Aquinas' influence that much of Western tradition since that time has been preoccupied with the personal salvation of humankind through Jesus. Today, however, it is Duns Scotus' position that is gaining ground. Jesus Christ is no after-thought; rather he is the culmination of all that God has created. He is God's first-intended through whom all things came to be. The declaration of Genesis that all is good finds its fulfilment in the words spoken on the occasion of Jesus' baptism: 'You are my Son, the Beloved; my favour rests on you.'

But, as we have already seen, the story of creation cannot be described simply as a marvellous celebratory event. It has been a story of struggle, destruction, waste, sinfulness, death and pain. And so, in making his home amongst us as our friend, Jesus also comes as our saviour, bringing healing to a world devastated and broken in so many ways. It is in Jesus that we come to know the full extent of God's goodness who loves to the end – to the point of death and beyond.

OUR NEED FOR JESUS AS SAVIOUR

Inevitable Suffering

There is so much suffering in our world which is beyond our control. Even if the whole world was brimful of love and goodwill, there would still be a huge area of pain and suffering. There are the tragic accidents that frequently befall us and those we love: natural disasters that strike down thousands and mysterious diseases so deadly to human life. There seems to be a brutal arbitrariness at the heart of creation which results in deformed children and whole communities devastated by earthquakes, mud-slides and flooding. It can hardly be surprising that such experiences obscure for many the possibility of a loving God.

A similar kind of helplessness is true of another range of human afflictions. Occasionally our job demands that we move from the people and the neighbourhood we love; many suffer the indignity and strain of redundancy; we see people unable to bear children and others who give birth to a handicapped child; all of us feel the weakness of illness or experience the shock of an accident; some of us undergo the discomfort and wretchedness of serious surgery. Stress, strain, failure and loneliness all too often dominate the journey of life. And then, of course, there is death itself. It is frequently set in tragic circumstances: in war, in famine, upon our streets; suddenly and unexpectedly, sometimes violently. It tears parents from children and breaks the embrace of husband and wife.

Suffering Caused by Sin

But there is another kind of suffering, perhaps even more traumatic, which arises directly from the evil within people's hearts. In this respect, the Nazi Holocaust stands as an indisputable sign of our capacity for evil. During this past century, so often characterised as one of unparalleled progress, we have witnessed suffering and death on a scale we can hardly imagine. Hell on earth has been conjured up by morbid and sadistic minds on the Somme, in the Gulag, at Dachau, and Auschwitz. Men, women, and children have been systematically brutalised; and, despite the lessons of history, there is continuing violation of human rights. It seems that we can never escape the passion, gazing upon the disfigured features of so many people caught up in the horror of gratuitous violence. Every day they are splashed unrelentingly on our television screens. Suffering and death seem to have unassailable power, an iron grip holding us in fear.

It would not seem too much of an exaggeration to say with St Augustine: 'From the time when our nature sinned in paradise . . . we have all become one lump of clay, a lump of sin. Since then, by sinning, we have forfeited our merit and God's mercy is withdrawn from us so that we sinners are owed nothing but eternal damnation.'[1] These words represent a fundamental truth of the scriptures: following the rebellion of Adam and Eve the whole of humanity has been damaged; there is a tragic flaw in our make-up. Violence has spread over the face of the earth with the terrifying consequences we have already described: 'All have sinned and fall short of the glory of God' (Romans 3:23). We have chosen greed, envy, deceit, resentment, and injustice, instead of love, truth, kindness, honesty and compassion. We have been caught up in the radical sinfulness of the human race, alienated from God, bearing division amongst ourselves. Sin, beginning within each of us, and then, striking at the heart of marriage and family life, has spread outwards to engulf whole nations. It is no wonder that Jesus should say, 'Cut off from me you can do nothing' (John 15:5). Everyone, without exception, is radically dependent upon the mercy and forgiveness of God. And so we must now trace the manner whereby the Father 'has rescued us from the ruling force of darkness and transferred us to the kingdom of the Son that he loves' (Colossians 1:13-14; cf Catechism pars. 396-412)

A GOD OF PASSION FOR HIS PEOPLE

The Cross at the Heart of Creation

'However much sin increased, grace was always the greater' (Romans 5:20). Those words of St Paul describe well the outpouring of God's love from the beginning. He constantly declares our world to be good; he creates men and women in his image and likeness to share love and companionship; following their sinfulness 'Yahweh God made tunics of skins for the man and his wife and clothed them' (Genesis 3:21); Eve soon gives birth to a child 'with the help of the Lord' (Genesis 4:2). Despite the rebellion of Adam and Eve, therefore, God never abandons them. He becomes their partner on life's journey, opening up a future for them, and constantly blessing them on their way. The same pattern is evident in the story of Cain and Abel. Cain refuses to acknowledge Abel as his brother and, to further his own selfish desires, murders him. And yet, 'Yahweh put a mark on Cain, so that no one coming across him would kill him' (Genesis 4:15). Once again, we have a sign of God's determination not to write us off. 'However much sin increased, grace was always the greater' (Romans 5:20).

God does take seriously the sinfulness of human violence and, on one occasion, seemed determined to put an end to it all: 'God said to Noah: 'I have decided that the end has come for all living things, for the earth is full of lawlessness because of human beings. So I am now about to destroy them and the earth' (Genesis 6:13). But because Noah was a righteous man, God had 'a change of heart' and promised that never again would he destroy every human creature (Genesis 8:21). The rainbow appeared in the clouds as a continuing sign of the passion of God for his people. From the very first moment, therefore, God has continually 'emptied himself', determined to save the world from its sins. 'Can a woman forget her baby at the breast, feel no pity for the child she has borne? Even if these were to forget, I shall not forget you' (Isaiah 49:15). In the course of time, the endlessly generous fidelity of God is made known in Jesus, the Beloved, who through his passion and death, loves to the end.

Suffered under Pontius Pilate

These few words, perhaps more than any others in the Creed, anchor the story of Jesus at a particular point and place in human history. Pontius Pilate was the Roman Governor of Judea from 26AD to 36AD under whom Jesus was put to death. We are familiar with a number of details concerning Pilate's involvement: in Matthew's account, Pilate is overwhelmed by the demand of the people for the crucifixion of Jesus and, in a dramatic gesture, publicly washes his hands: 'I am innocent of this man's blood. It is your concern' (Matthew 27:25); and in John's account Pilate affirms the kingship of Jesus in all the languages of the Empire, despite the objections of the Jewish chief priests: 'What I have written, I have written' (John 19:22). But, most of all, the mention of Pilate in the Creed is important because it marks that point in the world's history when God made known the extent of his love for us in the horrifying death of Jesus by crucifixion.

Jesus *suffered* under Pontius Pilate: He experienced rejection by whole cities (Matthew 11:24), including his home town of Nazareth (Mark 6:4) and his own disciples (John 6:67). Towards the end of his life we find Jesus troubled and in doubt about his ability to go through with the suffering and death which were approaching: 'My Father, if it be possible, let this cup pass me by' (Matthew 26:39). When the moment arrived, he experienced the full horror of his own painful death, after his life had seemingly collapsed around him in total failure, with his message reduced to absurdity: 'Save yourself: come down from the cross! He saved others, he cannot save himself . . . let him come down from the cross now, for us to see it and believe' (Mark 15:30). In fear and trembling, he now turns to the Father in whom he placed so much trust: 'My God, my God, why have you forsaken me?' (Mark 15:34). The Father, however, remained silent and did not intervene. In that moment of darkness, Jesus experienced total helplessness and saw himself as a complete failure. In doing so, he embraced all men and women who are wounded deeply in life – through bereavement, a failed marriage, an incurable disease – sharing with them that sense of abandonment, the terrible fear that their lives are without meaning. Jesus entered into their situation of loneliness and embraced them there with the outstretched arms of the crucified.

Crucified, Died, and was Buried

• *The experience of crucifixion*

We are familiar with crosses and crucifixes. We find them in churches, on altars, on buildings, in cemeteries, on flags. We bless ourselves with the sign of the cross during public worship or at private prayer. Everywhere we are reminded of the way Jesus died. And yet, their familiarity can make us immune to the harsh reality they represent. This is particularly true when the cross is worn by so many simply as a piece of jewelry, with little or no understanding of its significance.

Death by crucifixion was a barbaric form of execution. It was often preceded by various kinds of torture, at least a flogging, before the victim carried the beam to the place of execution. There he would be nailed to the beam with outstretched arms, raised up and seated on a small wooden peg. Then, there would follow the long drawn out torments of hanging on the cross, before death brought merciful release by asphyxiation. As a form of execution it gets close to being unbearable in its horror. Such was the experience of Jesus, put to death as a common criminal in a cruel and contemptible way.

• *'According to the scriptures' (cf Catechism pars. 599-605)*

Why did Jesus have to die in such a way? What hostile forces combined to bring about his crucifixion? Indeed, did Jesus have to suffer and die in this way? We are reminded of those passages in the Scriptures where Jesus speaks of the fate that awaited him: 'The Son of man will be delivered into the power of men; they will put him to death; and three days after he has been put to death he will rise again' (Mark 9:31). And we recall the reproach to the disciples on the road to Emmaus: 'Was it not necessary that the Christ should suffer before entering into his glory?' (Luke 24:26). It would seem that the death of Jesus was inevitable: he had to suffer, he had to be rejected, he had to be killed; it all happened 'in accordance with the Scriptures' (1 Corinthians 15:3, cf Luke 24:27).

By way of explanation, a striking passage from the writings of Plato might well provide a clue, when it describes the inevitable fate of a just and innocent man: 'The just man will be scourged, tortured, and imprisoned, his eyes will be put out, and after enduring every humiliation he will be crucified.'[2] These words suggest that Jesus died because of the unavoidable conflict between the goodness within him and the sinfulness of the human condition which closed in upon him. Indeed, he was increasingly aware that his life would have a violent end. He recalled the murder of so many prophets who had gone before him (Luke 11:47); and, in the parable of the wicked tenants, when he spoke of the killing of the beloved son, he undoubtedly referred to the fate that awaited him (Mark 12:6). Jesus willingly and knowingly went to his death, refusing to abandon his mission from the Father even to save his own life.

• *The opponents of Jesus*

Over the centuries, Christians have unjustly accused *Jews* of the crime of deicide because of their involvement in the crucifixion of Jesus. On a simplistic reading, such an accusation would seem to have some basis in the Passion narratives. Matthew, for example, writes: 'And the people, everyone of them, shouted back: "Let his blood be upon us and on our children!"' (Matthew 27:25); and John, throughout his Gospel, speaks of the Jews in an hostile way (cf John 19:12ff). These passages, however, must not justify continuing hostility between Christians and Jews. In the words of the Second Vatican Council:

> 'True, authorities of the Jews and those who followed their lead pressed for the death of Christ (cf John 19:6); still, what happened in his Passion cannot be blamed on all the Jews then living, without distinction, nor upon the Jews of today. Although the Church is the new People of God, the Jews should not be presented as repudiated or cursed by God, as if such views followed from the Holy Scriptures'[3] (cf Catechism 597). Rather, 'Christian sinners are more to blame for the death of Christ than those few Jews who brought it about – they indeed "knew not what they did"'[4] (cf Catechism 598).

Focussing now upon the specific circumstances of Jesus' ministry, it has often been assumed that the *Pharisees* were the principal opponents of Jesus because of the way in which Jesus so bitterly criticised their leadership: 'Hypocrites! How rightly Isaiah prophesied about you when he said: "This people honours me only with lip-service, while their hearts are far from me"' (Matthew 15:8ff). And yet there is no explicit mention of the Pharisees when Jesus is being tried which suggests that nothing about Jesus motivated them to become involved in his execution.[5]

More significant, perhaps, were the *Sadducees* who were most concerned to protect the essential features of Jewish life, especially those traditions associated with the Temple. They would be threatened in several ways by Jesus. They accused him of being a blasphemer, not only because of his cleansing the Temple and foretelling its destruction, but because he placed his preaching and the kingdom of God above the authority of Moses and the Law. He broke the Sabbath commandment and the Jewish ritual purity regulations; he associated with sinners at table and extended to them a forgiveness which could only come from God; and he frequently placed himself above the law of Moses, claiming to act with the authority of his Father. Because he offered such a threat to the survival of Judaism he had to be silenced once and for all. As Caiaphas said: 'It is to your advantage that one man should die for the people, rather than that the whole nation should perish' (John 11:50; cf Catechism par. 595).

But, as we have seen, Jesus was actually put to death by the *Romans*. At that time, as in so many situations today, it would be impossible to separate the religious from the political. In many respects, Jesus was closely associated with the 'Zealots': like them, he preached that the kingdom of God was at hand; there is no record of him condemning the Zealots; he had in his company at least one disciple described as a Zealot; and his own disciples certainly understood his mission in terms of setting Israel free (Luke 24:21). But Jesus did not preach the violent overthrow of the Roman occupiers. On the contrary, he preached that we must love our enemies which would have been judged outrageous by the Zealots. Nevertheless, the full impact of Jesus' ministry created at least the danger of a new popular revolt and so he was rejected as a blasphemer and condemned as a rebel.

• *Jesus' experience of the cross*

The real reason, however, which brought Jesus to the cross is given by St Luke. He interprets the passion and death of Jesus as the story of one who said with his dying breath:

'Father, into your hands I commit my spirit' (Luke 23:46). In suffering and dying upon the cross, Jesus was fulfilling perfectly the will of his Father. So insistent is St Luke upon this point that he presents his whole Gospel account in terms of Jesus' journey towards Jerusalem: 'Now it happened that, as the time drew near for him to be taken up, he resolutely turned his face towards Jerusalem' (9:51). Jesus must go up to Jerusalem because it is there that the promises of God, repeated so often through the prophets (Isaiah 40:1-2; Zephaniah 3:14-15), must be fulfilled. Jerusalem is none other than the dwelling place of God. Only there could it be seen that Jesus was faithful to the end.

Such faithfulness brought Jesus to an experience of torture and humiliating execution. When he passed from the upper room to the garden of Gethsemane he began to feel that sense of isolation which would reach its climax in the cry of abandonment on the cross. His mood of sadness and anxiety is summed up in the words: 'My soul is sorrowful to the point of death' (Matthew 26:38). All consolation is taken away. Jesus shrinks from the cup which he must drink. The Father, to whom he has been so faithful, begins to hide his face and remains so silent. There is no anticipation of Easter to comfort him. His life, it seems, has collapsed around him in total disaster. He is now to be betrayed into the hands of sinners (Mark 14:41). He is confronted by the Jewish authorities, Pilate, Herod, brutal soldiers, and mocking crowds. He is let down by those even closest to him: Judas betrayed him, Peter denied him three times, and the rest of the apostles abandoned him in his time of need. Most of all, Jesus experienced the absence of the one whose presence he could most have expected: 'My God, my God, why have you forsaken me?' (Mark 15:34; cf Catechism pars. 606-618).

Jesus experienced death as the absolute darkness of hell. He felt the full weight of abandonment and rejection by the Father. On the cross he was confronted with the reality of sin in all its naked horror. Such is one important meaning of the phrase in our creed, *he descended into hell*. It seeks to affirm the full reality of the death of Jesus, indicating that there is no depth, no darkness, untouched by the Son of God.[6]

But we know in faith that this darkness was not the ultimate fact of Jesus' existence. The ultimate fact is the great love which prompted him, in the midst of his darkness, to say to another who was crucified with him: 'In truth I tell you, today you will be with me in paradise' (Luke 23:43), and to utter with confidence: 'Father, into your hands I commit my spirit' (Luke 23:46). These words speak of the incomprehensible power of his love which filled the moment of his death and overcame the power of hell. Such an appreciation of his death, however, can only be made known to us in the light of the resurrection.

On the Third Day He Rose Again

The proclamation that Christ is risen belongs to the heart of the Christian message. In the words of St Paul: 'If Christ has not been raised, then our preaching is without substance, and so is your faith . . . if our hope in Christ has been for this life only, we are of all people ˌthe most pitiable' (1 Corinthians 15:14,19). But even so, how did a new beginning come about after such a disastrous end? When Jesus died, it seemed for the disciples that the world had come to an end. Peter had denied all knowledge of Jesus and the rest had fled in disarray. They were people for whom God had no meaning and for whom death alone reigned (Luke 24:20). And yet, what a transformation! Those same disciples, the scared fugitives of Good Friday, became courageous preachers of the Gospel: 'God raised this man Jesus to life, and of that we are all witnesses' (Acts 2:36). In this announcement they proclaimed that something radically new, and totally unexpected, had taken place concerning God and the whole world. It is not surprising, therefore, that they should find difficulty putting this new experience into words. And so, in the New Testament, we find many images and stories which seek to do justice to the resurrection experience. One such story is that of the empty tomb.

The Empty Tomb (cf Catechism par. 640)

All the Gospel accounts testify that Mary Magdalene with one or more female companions found the tomb to be open and that the body of Jesus had mysteriously disappeared. Some look upon this testimony as irrefutable proof of the resurrection, whilst others look upon the empty tomb as an irrelevance. How must we assess the importance of the empty tomb?

It must, first of all, be admitted that our faith in the resurrection of Jesus does not depend upon the testimony concerning the empty tomb. The simple fact of the empty tomb is ambiguous and open to a number of possible explanations. One story circulating at the time suggested that the disciples stole the body of Jesus. And so, all that is conveyed by the empty tomb is that 'He is not here'. This falls far short of the conviction 'He is risen'.

Nevertheless, testimony concerning the empty tomb remains, stubbornly, at an extremely early level of the tradition about the resurrection. It cannot be discarded. And we have no evidence that anyone, either Christian or non-Christian, ever suggested that the body of Jesus still remained within the tomb. Indeed, had they produced the body of Jesus, it would have been impossible for the disciples to proclaim his resurrection in Jerusalem.

But how does the empty tomb give support to our Easter faith? First of all, it serves to establish that the risen Lord is none other than the crucified Jesus. Secondly, the emptiness of the tomb reflects the newness of life which Jesus now enjoys: death no longer has any power over him; all manner of corruption has been overcome. And thirdly, the empty tomb says something about the way in which the whole life of Jesus in his earthly body has been taken up into his glorious risen life. Nothing is wasted. Other stories, however, speak more powerfully of the resurrection experience, especially the stories concerning the appearance of the risen Lord to his disciples.

The Appearances of the Risen Lord (cf Catechism pars. 641-645)

A striking feature of the Gospel accounts of the appearances of the risen Lord is the tremendous discrepancy among the stories. Some writers say that Jesus appeared in Galilee, whilst others say he appeared in Jerusalem. Some emphasise the continuity of the risen Lord with the person the disciples knew before his death: 'Put your finger here; look here are my hands. Give me your hand; put it into my side. Do not be unbelieving any more but believe' (John 20:27); and again: 'Touch me and see for your selves; a ghost has no flesh and bones as you can see I have . . . and they offered him a piece of grilled fish, which he took and ate before their eyes' (Luke 24:42). Others emphasise the newness of life which Jesus now enjoys as risen Lord: 'And their eyes were opened and they recognised him; but he had vanished from their sight' (Luke 24:31); and again: 'The doors were closed, but Jesus came in and stood among them' (John 20:26).

Despite these discrepancies, however, we can be assured of the following:

> Shortly after the death of Jesus, a number of disciples, who had witnessed the death of Jesus, had experiences which convinced them that the same Jesus was alive and present amongst them.

> They were convinced that these experiences were due to an act of power by God: 'the whole House of Israel can be certain that the Lord and Christ whom God has made is this Jesus whom you crucified' (Acts 2:36).

> They were able to identify the risen Lord as none other than Jesus of Nazareth, the one they all had known

before his death: 'And their eyes were opened and they recognised him' (Luke 24:31).

They frequently describe their experience in terms of 'seeing' the Lord: 'So Mary of Magdala told the disciples, "I have seen the Lord"' (John 20:18). But this 'seeing' is only possible through the eyes of faith. No neutral observers could have made contact with the risen Lord.

They experienced a profound transformation, from being cowardly and timid in the face of Jesus' death, to being courageous preachers of the Gospel, refusing to waver despite all manner of intimidation.

Perhaps this transformation holds the real key to the truth of the resurrection of Jesus.

'And We Are All Witnesses'

We have already noted that the disciples were totally unprepared for the resurrection of Jesus. When Jesus died, their world came to an end. All hope had disappeared as they journeyed away from Jerusalem. And yet, within a very short space of time, these same people are returning to the streets of Jerusalem preaching with boldness that God had raised from the dead the one who had been crucified (Acts 2:22-36; 3:12-15). They are threatened with punishment and imprisonment; they are prepared to die for their message. They do not waver: 'We cannot stop proclaiming what we have seen and heard' (Acts 4:21). Such a transformation could not possibly be based upon wishful thinking, or upon some hallucinatory experience. It is only the risen Lord, the one who died never to die again, who could be responsible for the change that overwhelmed them. They could point to the empty tomb; but they could not point to the body of the risen Lord beside them. All they could say was: 'God raised this man Jesus to life, and of that we are all witnesses' (Acts 2:33). In other words, 'Look at us and then you will know that what we say is true.' We should now consider a little more closely the message entrusted to them and its meaning for today.

The Message of Easter

The early proclamation of the Gospel, as we find it in the Acts of the Apostles, made little or no reference to the death of Jesus upon the cross. Its principal focus was upon the resurrection: 'It was the God of our ancestors who raised up Jesus, whom you executed by hanging on a tree' (Acts 5:30). Although there are passing references to Jesus' death being in some way according to the scriptures (Acts 4:11), it was not reckoned to be part of the Gospel. Rather, it was looked upon as a most unfortunate, tragic, event that should never have happened. But now it does not matter, because that same Jesus has been raised from the dead and is present amongst us.

It soon became clear, however, that more consideration should be given to the significance of the death of Jesus. This was done by St Paul when he was forced to explain why those who believed still suffered and died. How can they accept the Lord's resurrection as Good News when they and their loved ones continue to suffer and to die? In fact their sufferings had become more intense since they had accepted Jesus as their Lord and Saviour.

And so St Paul begins to reflect upon the *death* of Jesus as part of the Good News. He first speaks of it in this way to a group of Thessalonians who are grieving because of the death of their loved ones: 'We believe that Jesus died and rose again, and that in the same way God will bring with him those who have fallen asleep in Jesus' (1 Thessalonians 4:14). It enables him, too, to speak of his own sufferings as an apostle: 'We are subjected to every kind of hardship, but never distressed; we see no way out but we never despair; we are pursued but never cut off; knocked down but still have some life in us; always we carry with us in our body the death of Jesus so that the life of Jesus, too, may be visible in our body' (2 Corinthians 4:8-10). For St Paul, it is Christ's death which changes the nature of the Christian's sufferings and death.

St Paul's attempt to explain how this happens touches the limits of human understanding and will always remain a mystery. But St Paul is saying that our sufferings and death are somehow joined with the sufferings and death of Christ; and because of that we too share in his resurrection. To express this intimate relationship between ourselves and Christ, St Paul uses a variety of prepositional phrases: 'I have been crucified *with* Christ and yet I am alive; yet it is no longer I, but Christ living *in* me' (Galatians 2:20). We are so intertwined with the experience of Christ that our sufferings are now essentially different; they are no longer a defeat but a victory. Because of Christ we can now cry: 'Death, where is your victory? Death, where is your sting?' (1 Corinthians 15:55).

St Paul has far from solved the mystery of our suffering, but he has helped us to look upon suffering in a totally new light. In communion with the risen Lord, the sufferings of people today, in Bosnia, in Northern Ireland, in Latin America and South Africa, in our own country, are inextricably caught up with his sufferings. Their crosses somehow become his; his cross becomes their crosses (Romans 6:3-4). This mystical truth, so central in the writings of St Paul, has given strength to countless Christians in their sufferings and helped to make sense of the bafflement of pain. They are given strength by knowing that Christ is with them. They are comforted by knowing that they can help others to experience the triumph of Jesus upon the cross. No matter how meaningless a particular situation may seem to be, no suffering is wasted, no tears are lost.

In many other ways, too, we are able to see around us the signs of death's final defeat: the grass blade thrusts up through barren sand; lilies glory in wasteland; fractured limbs heal; broken lives mend; wounds become scars. We see it, too, in the skilled attention of doctors and nurses as they bring people back from the brink of death; in the courage of men and women who risk their lives protesting against the mindless violence which surrounds us. So many signs of a permanent future, of resurrection. It is the ascension which seals that future forever.

HE ASCENDED INTO HEAVEN

At the end of the gospel according to St Luke, the Ascension of Jesus is described in simple terms: 'Now as (Jesus) blessed them, he withdrew from them and was carried up to heaven' (Luke 24:51). In the Acts of the Apostles, on the other hand, it is presented in more graphic detail: 'As he said this he was lifted up while they looked on, and a cloud took him from their sight' (Acts 1:9).

However we are to understand the manner of the ascension, it marks the end of a period of time during which the apostles and others of the disciples had privileged experiences of the risen Lord. St Luke refers to a period of 'forty days' (Acts 1:3), evoking memories of Israel's 'forty years' in the desert before entering the Promised Land, and Jesus' 'forty days' in the desert before embarking on his public ministry. The number 'forty', therefore, is not to be interpreted literally; rather, it is a device intended by Luke to mark the beginning of the life and mission of the Christian community. These meetings with the risen Lord gradually enabled the disciples to understand all that he had said to them, all that he had done with them. Now the time has come for Jesus to return to the Father. Never again will he walk with them on the streets of Palestine, healing the sick and preaching about the kingdom of God. His mission has now been completed.

But more needs to be said about the significance of the ascension. In many passages of the New Testament we read of Jesus being 'exalted to the right hand of the Father' (Acts 2:33; 7:55-56; Romans 8:34). But one passage above all impresses upon us the position now enjoyed by Jesus: 'God raised him high, and gave him the name which is above all other names; so that all beings in the heavens, on earth and in the underworld, should bend the knee at the name of Jesus and that every tongue should acknowledge Jesus Christ as Lord, to the glory of God the Father' (Philippians 2:9-11). We can now approach the throne of grace with confidence (Hebrews 4:16); we now have access to the Holy of Holies. We should not let go of this confidence too easily. Because Jesus is now ascended, and has returned to the Father from whom he came, the love and mercy of God are final: 'Nothing . . . will be able to come between us and the love of God, known to us in Christ Jesus our Lord' (Romans 8:39). The apostles must now share with others what they themselves have received. But, first, they must be empowered to do so by the power of the Spirit (cf Catechism pars. 659-664).

NOTES

1 E Yarnold, *The Theology of Original Sin* (Mercier Press 1971), pp. 55-56
2 *Republic, Book II,* cited by Roderick Strange, *The Catholic Faith* (Oxford 1987), p. 24
3 Vatican II: *Nostra Aetate* par 4
4 *Notes on the Correct Way to Present the Jews and Judaism in Preaching and Catechesis in the Roman Catholic Church* (1985), par. 22
5 B C McDermott, *Word Become Flesh* (Liturgical Press 1993), p. 77
6 cf Catechism pars. 632-635: 'Christ went into the depths of death so that "the dead will hear the voice of the Son of God, and those who hear will live"' (John 5:25)

FURTHER READING

Catechism of the Catholic Church: pars. 571-678
McDermott Brian, *Word Become Flesh* (Liturgical Press 1993)
O'Collins, Gerald, *Interpreting Jesus*, (Chapman 1983)
O'Donnell, John, *Hans Urs von Balthasar* (Chapman 1992)
Strange, Roderick, *The Catholic Faith* (OUP 1986)
Taylor, John V, *The Christlike God* (SCM 1992)

CHAPTER SIX

I BELIEVE IN THE HOLY SPIRIT

IDENTIFYING THE SPIRIT

It is commonplace to remark upon the difficulty of defining spirit; but there is no mistaking its presence. And so, for example, there is no mistaking the difference between two people simply travelling together on the same bus and two others of whom we can say, 'There's a marvellous spirit between them.' Again, we can go into a school, and after just a short time say, 'There's an excellent spirit in that school.' We cannot see the spirit that makes the difference but we can certainly sense it. It is the spirit that gives the spark, brings to life, and makes the connection.

This explains why the apostles had no difficulty identifying those who had not yet received the Spirit. And so, in Acts 8:14-17, after the conversion of a number of people in Samaria, Peter and John went there and prayed for the Samaritans to receive the Holy Spirit: 'For as yet he had not come down on any of them: they had only been baptised in the name of the Lord Jesus.' A little later, in Acts 19:1-7, St Paul finds people at Ephesus who had only received John's baptism, and had not heard that there was a Holy Spirit. And finally, writing to the Corinthians, St Paul tells them that 'no one can say "Jesus is Lord", except by the Holy Spirit' (1 Corinthians 12:3). Anyone, of course, can utter these words, but they only become an act of faith through the presence of the Spirit of God.

NEGLECT OF THE HOLY SPIRIT

Until more recent times, as we have already mentioned, the Holy Spirit has long been the forgotten person of the Trinity.

There have been many reasons for this lapse in the 'memory' of the Church's tradition.

> It is much easier to relate to the Father and the Son because by their very names they present to us a 'face'. Through the life and ministry of Jesus we have come to know something of the 'personality' of the Father as compassionate and caring for each one of us. The Spirit, on the other hand, is only accessible to us through a variety of symbols such as wind, breath, fire, water, the finger of God, and a dove (cf Catechism 694-701).

> Contrary to the experience of the New Testament, where we read of the overwhelming, shattering experience of the Spirit, Catholic tradition has insisted for more than four centuries that we could not have a direct knowledge of the state of grace. Deprived of a sense of the power of the Spirit of God in our lives, for many of us religion deteriorated into a lifeless and dreary system of rules and ceremonies.

> As a consequence, we lost our sense of Christian fellowship. Our religion was very much a 'God and me' affair and, generally, we were quite oblivious to those around. Most of us will remember the rules given to us as children for proper conduct in church or when at prayer: no unnecessary talking and no laughing, kneeling with eyes cast down and hands joined together. Far from being a fellowship of loving believers, conscious of being bound together in the one Spirit, we were strangers to one another. Inevitably, in such circumstances, we were suspicious of all movements of enthusiasm.

An Orthodox bishop has pointed to some of the terrible consequences which come from a neglect of the Spirit:

'Without the Holy Spirit, God is far away, Christ
stays in the past, the Gospel is a dead letter, the
Church is simply an organisation . . . But in the
Holy Spirit: the world is resurrected and groans
with the birth pangs of the kingdom, the risen
Christ is there, the Gospel is the power of life,
the Church shows forth the life of the Trinity,
mission is a Pentecost . . .'[1]

In recent times, strong voices are being raised within the
Christian Churches testifying to the importance of recovering
a sense of the Spirit in our lives. And so, as the Second
Vatican Council opened, Pope John XXIII prayed that the
Church might experience a new Pentecost; later, Pope Paul
VI continued that prayer, emphasising that 'the Church needs
her perennial Pentecost; she needs fire in her heart, words on
her lips, prophecy in her outlook. She needs to be the Temple
of the Spirit';[2] and more recently, Pope John Paul II in his
encyclical on the Holy Spirit (1986) called for a new study of
and devotion to the Holy Spirit.

The most significant development, however, must surely
be the dramatic emergence of the 'charismatic renewal' that
first spread like fire among the Protestant Churches in 1956
and in the Roman Catholic Church in 1967. Prayer Groups
emerged as a characteristic feature of the Church's life; an
ever-increasing number of people began to experience the
presence of God in a totally new way – no longer as a vague,
distant figure on the periphery of their lives, but a God whose
unconditional love they felt at the centre of their lives and
thought. They experienced in a striking way the truth of those
words of Ezekiel: 'I shall give you a new heart, and put a
new spirit in you; I shall remove the heart of stone from
your bodies and give you a heart of flesh instead' (Ezekiel
36:26).

It is this understanding of the loving presence of God in
the Spirit penetrating human experience which is taken so
utterly for granted in the pages of the Scriptures.

THE SPIRIT OF GOD IN THE SCRIPTURES

(CATECHISM PARS. 702-730)

The Creative Spirit of God

We first meet the Spirit of God at the very beginning of the Bible. The whole of creation takes place under the presidency of the hovering Spirit of God when the waters of chaos are transformed into the wonders of creation (Genesis 1:2). In the second creation story, the creation of man is the climax when God breathes his own breath into him so that he becomes a living being (Genesis 2:7). From that moment, the Spirit of God is always at work in nature, in history, in human living; and wherever there is breakdown in God's handiwork, he is present to renew and create again.

> 'In the ravines you opened up springs,
> running down between the mountains,
> supplying water for all the wild beasts .. ;
> for cattle you make the grass grow,
> and for people the plants they need,
> to bring forth food from the earth . . .
> Turn away your face and they panic;
> turn back their breath and they die
> and revert to dust.
> Send out your breath and life begins;
> you renew the face of the earth.' (Psalm
> 104:10,15,28-30)

The Prophetic Spirit of God

This same Spirit at work in the whole of creation makes his presence felt in the lives of individuals. Moses meets God at the top of the mountain in the midst of a storm (Exodus 19:18); Elijah, on the other hand, finds God in a tiny whispering sound (1 Kings 19:9-13). The great prophets are conscious of being possessed by the Spirit, enabling them to speak the truth of God with clarity of vision and great courage in the face of personal danger and, not infrequently, death itself. It is from the prophet Ezekiel that we receive the most dramatic vision of the power of the Spirit:

> 'Prophesy over these bones. Say "Dry bones hear the word of Yahweh. The Lord Yahweh says this to these bones: I am now going to make the breath enter you, and you will live. I shall put sinews on you, I shall make flesh grow on you. I shall cover you with skin and give you breath, and you will live; and you will learn that I am Yahweh."' (Ezekiel 37:4-6)

The Experience of God in the Spirit

God's Spirit, then, is the source of all life, penetrating every aspect of creation, breaking down barriers, securing freedom from all manner of oppression, enabling springs to gush forth from desert places. In particular, God's spirit works powerfully in the hearts of human beings, made in his image and likeness.

It is no wonder, therefore, that this experience should find expression in terms of the relationship between a husband and wife who are deeply in love. It is regarded as the only adequate language in which to express the warmth and affection of the presence of God's love. And so in the prophecy of Hosea we read:

> 'I shall betroth you to myself for ever, I shall betroth you in uprightness and justice, and faithful love and tenderness. Yes, I shall betroth you to myself in loyalty and in the knowledge of Yahweh. I shall tell Lo-Ammi, "You are my people", and he will say, "You are my God".' (Hosea 2:16-22)

This same theme is developed in a most remarkable way in the Song of Songs, a collection of love poems included in the

Bible to express the relationship between God and his
people.

> 'I hear my love. See how he comes leaping on the
> mountains, bounding over the hills. My beloved
> is like a gazelle, like a young stag . . . My love lifts
> up his voice, he says to me, "Come, then, my
> beloved, my lovely one come".' (Song of Songs
> 2:8-10)

In other words, God's love for his people is no less
tangible than the ecstatic love between husband and wife:
'Love is as strong as death, passion as relentless as Sheol. The
flash of it is a flash of fire, a flame of Yahweh himself. Love no
flood can quench, no torrents drown' (8:6-7).

God's Spirit in Jesus

The New Testament continues this theme of the life-giving
Spirit, first in relation to Jesus, and after his death and
resurrection, in relation to his followers. In Luke, the mother
of Jesus is overshadowed by the Spirit (Luke 1:35). Her
barren womb resembles the chaos over which the Spirit
hovered when God first uttered his creative word. It is by the
power of the same Spirit that Jesus is baptised by John in the
waters of the Jordan: 'And at once, as he was coming out of
the water, he saw the heavens torn apart and the Spirit, like a
dove, descending on him. And a voice came from heaven,
"You are my Son, the Beloved; my favour rests on you"'
(Mark 1:10-11). In this moment, Jesus not only experiences
himself being cherished as Son of the Father, but he also
becomes acutely conscious of the mission entrusted to him as
the 'Anointed One' in the Spirit (cf Catechism par. 690).

So, Jesus was driven out into the wilderness to prepare for
his critical confrontation with Satan whom he was to
encounter throughout his life. According to Luke, he
emerged from this encounter with renewed vigour, making his
own the words of Isaiah: 'The Spirit of the Lord is on me . . .

to bring the good news to the afflicted. He has sent me, to proclaim liberty to captives, sight to the blind, to let the oppressed go free' (Luke 4:18-19). Empowered by the Spirit, Jesus embarks upon his public ministry which will ultimately bring him to his death upon the cross. Indeed, the real baptism of Jesus is his death. And so we read in Luke 12:50: 'There is a baptism I must still receive, and what constraint I am under until it is completed.' And again in Mark 10:38: 'But Jesus said to them "You do not know what you are asking. Can you drink the cup that I shall drink, or be baptised with the baptism with which I must be baptised?"'

In death, Jesus symbolised total helplessness, impossibility in its most acute and final form. And yet, because Jesus remained totally faithful to his Father's will, the Spirit once more, and this time definitively, transformed chaos into life. Jesus, crucified in weakness, is raised by the Spirit of God. It is now that we know the Father received that final prayer of Jesus: 'Father, into your hands I commend my spirit.' As St John remarks during Jesus' public life: '. . . there was no Spirit as yet because Jesus had not been glorified' (John 7:39). But now, in the event of the cross, the Spirit, the inner life of God, is released and poured out for all of us, filling our hearts and our world with his presence (Catechism 728-730).

Experience of the Spirit of Christ

The first experience of the release of the Spirit was on the day of Pentecost. Luke describes this transformation in the coming of the Holy Spirit on the apostles in the form of fire. The Pentecostal experience (Acts 2:1-4) meant that fire entered into the disciples with the coming of the Spirit, a fire of such intensity that their lives were dramatically transformed, and they became courageous witnesses for Christ. The people around could only imagine that they were drunk but in fact they were intoxicated, not with wine, but with the devouring fire of the living God.

The early Christians, following upon this dramatic opening, were able to speak so naturally of the Spirit living and working amongst them. When the Christians in Jerusalem prayed for courage to speak the Gospel message, 'the house where they assembled rocked; they were all filled with the Holy Spirit and began to proclaim the word of God boldly' (Acts 4:31). The Spirit is recognised immediately in the tremendous transformation that it brought about in people's lives:

> 'I am continually thanking God about you, for the grace of God which you have been given in Christ Jesus; in him you have been richly endowed in every kind of utterance and knowledge; so firmly has witness to Christ taken root in you. And so you are not lacking in any gift as you wait for our Lord Jesus Christ to be revealed.' (1 Corinthians 1:4-8)

Above all, the Spirit enabled them to experience God's overwhelming love for them: 'What you received was not the spirit of slavery to bring you back into fear; you received the spirit of adoption, enabling us to cry out, "Abba, Father!"' (Romans 8:15-16).

With St Paul, the whole of the New Testament witness confirms the Spirit as a living, vibrant presence in peoples lives. They came to know as they had never known before the personal presence of God in the Spirit of Jesus Christ. Indeed, it is only through the release of the Spirit that they come to know the full power of Christ who gave himself up out of love for the Father for the salvation of all.

VOICES OF TRADITION

The Council of Constantinople (381) (Catechism par. 245)

After the Council of Nicaea in which the Church definitively rejected Arianism, affirming that the Son was fully equal with the Father, the Church turned its attention to the Holy Spirit. Since biblical times, trinitarian formulae were in constant use in the Church's liturgy, especially in the celebration of baptism. But now, the Church was called upon to clarify its understanding of the nature of the Holy Spirit and the relation of the Spirit to the Father and the Son.

In this respect, the contribution of St Athanasius (c. 360) was crucial. He argued that the Spirit is the spirit of Christ within us, and so, just as Jesus is divine so must the Spirit be divine. Furthermore, our salvation in Christ depends upon the work of the Spirit; it is the Spirit who makes Christ present to us and enables us to share his life; and so, once again, we must affirm that the Spirit is divine. In a famous text, Athanasius wrote:

> 'The Holy Spirit is the ointment and the seal with which the Word anoints and signs everything . . . Every time we say that we are partakers of Christ and partakers of God, we mean that that unction and that seal which is in us . . . is of the Son, who joins us to the Father by the Spirit who is in him. If the Holy Spirit were a creature, there could be no communion of God with us through him.'

Under the influence of Athanasius, the Council of Constantinople in 381 proclaimed: 'We believe in the Holy Spirit, the Lord and Giver of life who proceeds from the Father, who together with the Father and the Son is adored and glorified'. This early confession of faith does not explicitly speak of the Spirit as divine; instead, it speaks of the Spirit as life-giver, sharing in the work of the Father as creator and in the mission of the Son as saviour. The Spirit, therefore, can be addressed as Lord and, together with the Father and Son, is worthy of adoration and glorification.

The Contribution of St Augustine

St Augustine wrote extensively on the Trinity in a work entitled *De Trinitate*, which he put together at different dates between 399 and 419. In his quest to do justice to the distinctive nature of the Spirit, he appeals to two insights which are central to his vision: the Spirit as 'gift' and the Spirit as 'love'.

• *The Spirit as Gift:*

This image of the Spirit is well founded in the New Testament. A favourite text of St Augustine is that of Romans 5:5 where St Paul speaks of the love which is not deceptive 'because the love of God has been poured into our hearts by the Holy Spirit which has been given us'. We receive this Spirit as gift from the Father by faith (Galatians 3:2; John 7:38ff) and by baptism (1 Corinthians 6:11) and so the Spirit dwells within us (Romans 8:9). This Spirit, too, is the gift of the Son, whereby we are assured he dwells within us as risen Lord (1 John 3:24). No longer need we be afraid because he will always be with us through the gift of the Spirit until the end of time.

Basing his argument on these texts, and on many others which could be cited, St Augustine employs to good effect the image of the Spirit as the *donum Dei*, the gift of God. And since no one can give what is not theirs to give, in the gift of the Spirit God gives nothing less than himself. The Giver and the Gift are identical. It is in the Spirit, therefore, that we come to know the full extent of God as self-giving, who in Jesus 'emptied himself, taking the form of a slave . . . accepting death, death on a cross' (Philippians 2:6-8). As the Nicene Creed puts it: 'We believe in the Holy Spirit, the Lord, the giver of life.'

• *The Spirit as Love*

The other important image used by St Augustine is that of love. He says that there are three in the Trinity: the lover, the beloved and the love itself. The Father is the lover who gives himself entirely to the Son; the Son is the beloved in whom the Father is well pleased; and the Spirit is nothing less than the communion of love between Father and Son. This communion of love, however, is not self-absorbed, closed in upon itself. If such were the case, it would be no love at all. Indeed, far from being self-absorbed, the innermost nature of God is to be self-giving. The Holy Spirit enables this communion of love, the inner life of God, to be poured out for all of us, filling our hearts and our world with its presence. The Holy Spirit is, as it were, the abundance of God, the sheer overflow of love and grace. And so, in the words of St John, we read simply: 'God is love'.

'Filioque': a point of disagreement (Catechism pars. 246-248)

The Orthodox Churches of the East and the Roman Catholic Church of the West finally parted company in the Middle Ages. In 1054, the Patriarch of Constantinople was excommunicated and, in 1204, Constantinople was destroyed by Crusaders. Obviously a great number of issues contributed to this tragic state of affairs. But one major issue was the introduction of the 'filioque' clause into the Western version of the Nicene Creed: 'The Spirit proceeds from the Father *and the Son*.' The Eastern Church regarded such an addition as unscriptural and lacking the authority of an ecumenical council. Where lies the difference between the two approaches?

Under the influence of St Augustine, the Western tradition has focussed upon the threefold internal structure of God. So it stresses first of all the communion between Father and Son, by saying that the Spirit proceeds from the Father and Son as the fruit of their love. The strength of this approach is that it stresses the relationship between the Son and the Spirit. Since the Spirit is always the Spirit of Christ, then, this must be true also of the inner life of God. A weakness, however, is that talk about God can seem a matter of pure speculation when isolated from the circumstances in which God has made his name known as Father, Son, and Holy Spirit.

The Eastern tradition, on the other hand, has stressed the Father as the origin and source of everything within the Trinity as made known to us in Jesus Christ. And so, by confessing the Spirit as 'he who proceeds from the Father', it affirms that he comes *from* the Father *through* the Son. The strength of this approach lies in the recognition that 'God' in the Bible means in the first instance God the Father. It is the Father who entrusts everything to the Son (Matthew 11:27); it is the Father who will send the Advocate, the Holy Spirit, in the name of Jesus (John 14:26). A weakness, however, is that it does not clarify the relationship of the Son to the Spirit, which is a principal concern of the Western approach.

It is a tragedy that such diversity has contributed to a schism of the Church between East and West. Today, the ecumenical challenge is to seek reconciliation on this matter. One possibility would be to drop the word *filioque* since it did not appear in the Creed confessed at Constantinople in 381, and was only gradually admitted into the Latin liturgy between the eighth and eleventh centuries. On the other hand, a more acceptable possibility may be to accept both traditions as complementary to each other within the unity of faith. This would seem to acknowledge the caution necessary when speaking of God who is always beyond whatever we can say of him.

The Witness of the Mystical Tradition

We have already mentioned that for much of Christian tradition the Holy Spirit was the forgotten person of the Trinity. It was generally assumed that grace could not make its presence felt in our conscious personal lives. The writings of the Mystics, therefore, are important because, during this same period of time, they emphasised the religious experience of the presence of God in the Spirit. For this reason, increasing numbers of Christians are reading the writings of the Mystics and finding there a commentary on their own experience of the Spirit.

• Guidance during aridity

The Mystics, first of all, warn against the dangers of searching for physical sensation and warm feelings that many expect to accompany the presence of God. If we are true disciples of Jesus then we can expect to have to undergo deep spiritual suffering as he did: 'During his life on earth, he offered up prayer and entreaty, with loud cries and tears, to the one who had the power to save him from death, and, winning a hearing by his reverence, he learnt obedience, Son though he was, through his sufferings' (Hebrews 5:7-8). Such was the experience of the great Mystics themselves and so they were able to give valuable advice on how to cope with it.

St John of the Cross, for example, had this to say: 'What we must do in the dark night is leave the soul free and unencumbered, at rest from knowledge and thought . . . be content to wait upon God peacefully, attentively, without anxiety, not straining to experience or perceive him.'[4] And in her fourteenth revelation, Julian of Norwich received these comforting words from Jesus:

> 'Pray inwardly, even if you do not enjoy it. It does good, though you feel nothing, see nothing. Yes, even though you think you are doing nothing. For when you are dry, sick, or weak, at such a time is your prayer most pleasing to me though you find little enough to enjoy in it. This is true of all believing prayer.'[5]

• Nevertheless, a transforming experience

At the heart of faith, however, is a transforming experience by the Spirit of God and this was wholeheartedly acknowledged by all the Mystics. Once again, St John of the Cross speaks for many when he writes:

> 'There occurs that most delicate touch of the Beloved which the soul feels at times, even when least expecting it, and which sets the heart on fire with love . . . Then the will, in an instant, like one roused from sleep, burns with the fire of love, longs for God, praises him and gives him thanks, worships and honours him, and prays to him in the sweetness of love.'[6]

And there is Bernard of Clairvaux (1090-1153), a marvellous reforming monk of the twelfth century, whose sermons on the Song of Songs were to have an impact on all subsequent mystical theology:

> 'No sooner had he entered me than he awakened my drowsy soul, he touched my stony heart. He removed whatever was unwholesome, he began to plant; he watered what was withered; he enlightened the dark recesses, opened what was locked; he set the ice ablaze . . . And so my soul did bless the Lord, and all that is within me did bless his holy name.'[7]

Those words of St Bernard have been echoed many times in our own day as the Church experiences anew the presence of the Spirit.

THE CHURCH RENEWED IN THE POWER OF THE SPIRIT

Loyalty to the Church

A Church renewed in the Spirit, first of all, has a claim upon our loyalty. In the words of John Paul II:

> 'The Church communicates to us the riches of life and grace entrusted to her. She generates us by baptism, feeds us with the sacraments and the word of God, prepares us for mission, and is the reason for our existence as Christians; one cannot love Christ without loving the Church which Christ loves; and to the extent that one loves the Church of Christ, he possesses the Holy Spirit.'
> Puebla Conference 1979

In such loyalty are we to find our essential vocation. It is the way Christ has provided for us to share his life.

This is not always easy because the Church of Christ is also the church of sinners and, as such, so often presents a serious obstacle to faith. We must remember, however, that we are the Church. We are all sinners and belong to all those within the Church who obscure the light of the Gospel by their own mediocrity. We need to be mindful of those words of Jesus: 'Let the one among you who is guiltless be the first to throw a stone at her' (John 8:7). We must all bear the burden of our community, and do so in confidence, because it is precisely within the sinful flesh of our existence that God is powerfully at work.

A Church Alive to the Gifts of the Spirit

Being transformed by the power of the Spirit is not just intended for the few but for all without exception whom Jesus has called to himself in the life of the Church. The God who made his home in our world in the person of Jesus Christ nearly two thousand years ago is active in people's lives today through his Spirit. He is nothing less than the God of Jesus Christ who came close to us in flesh and blood to be seen and touched. When he was touched in faith, lives were changed (Luke 6:19; 8:44). This same Jesus is present to us today in the Spirit and it is in the Church above all that we should be able to reach and experience for ourselves the healing touch of God himself. In communion with Jesus, we are drawn by the Spirit into a deep and personal union with the Father and with one another.

It is in the Spirit that we become aware of the immense richness of the gifts of the Spirit. We are familiar with the principal gifts: love, joy, peace, patience, kindness, goodness, faithfulness, humility and self-control. Such gifts are available to all: the poor and the young, the rich and the old, men and women, the simple and the experts. Even though all may have different capacities, desires or abilities, beyond all these diversities everyone shares in the one Spirit. What is required is that we breathe new life into one another, create an experience of friendship with one another, draw out from one another what is best in each of us. Only in this way will we be able to help one another be rooted in the Spirit.

A Church Committed to Mission

As Christians rooted in the Spirit, we are called to be witnesses to the Gospel of Jesus Christ, instinctively sharing with others what we have received. This means, first of all, possessing a deeply rooted conviction of being totally accepted and cherished by God as Father; recognising Jesus as the Lord of our life; and experiencing the Spirit praying within, bringing alive the love that comes from Father and Son.

In the Spirit, the risen Lord is present; the Gospel is no longer a dead letter; the Church is a communion of believers made one by the power of the Father, Son and Holy Spirit; the liturgy is truly an occasion for celebration. This vivid awareness of the Father, of Jesus as Lord, and of the Spirit, brings home in a remarkable way the love, care, guidance, power, mercy and providence of God. No evangelisation is possible without such personal conversion: 'The world is calling for evangelisers to speak to it of a God whom the evangelists themselves should know and be familiar with as if they could see the invisible.'[8]

Filled with the Spirit, we cannot be indifferent to so many millions of people who constantly live with hunger, many of them dying of malnutrition. For the Spirit we receive is none other than the Spirit of Jesus Christ who was so passionate in his concern for the poor (Luke 4:18). Indeed, it is the continuing mission of the Spirit of Jesus Christ gradually to draw the whole of creation back to the Father. In the words of St Paul: 'We are well aware that the whole creation, until this time, has been groaning in labour pains. And not only that: we too, who have the first-fruits of the Spirit, even we are groaning inside ourselves, waiting with eagerness for our bodies to be set free' (Romans 8:22-24; cf Gaudium et Spes no. 22).

Note: Some material in this chapter is taken from the chapter on Confirmation in the author's book, *Focus on Sacraments*, (Mayhew 1987).

NOTES

1 cited by Kenneth Leach in *True God* (SPCK 1985), p. 199
2 cited in E Connor, *Pope Paul and the Spirit* (Ave Maria Press 1978)
   p. 183
3. cited by J J O'Donnell, *The Mystery of the Triune God* (Sheed & Ward
   1988), p. 76
4 St John of the Cross, *Dark Night of the Soul*, I,V,i-I,X,iv, cited by
   E Hamilton, *The Voice of the Spirit* (DLT 1976), pp. 68-69
5 Julian of Norwich, *Revelations of Divine Love* (Penguin 1974),
   pp. 124-125
6 St John of the Cross, *Spiritual Canticle 8*, cited in C O'Connor,
   Contemplationand Charismatic Renewal, in *Doctrine and Life* 1976, p. 707
7 St Bernard of Clairvaux, *Sermons on the Song of Songs*, no. 74
8 Pope Paul VI, *On Evangelisation*, no. 76

FURTHER READING

Catechism of the Catholic Church: pars. 687-741
Harrington, Wilfrid, *Spirit of the Living God* (Michael Glazier 1977)
Lash, Nicholas, *Believing Three Ways in One God* (SCM 1992)
Leech, Kenneth, *True God* (SCM 1987)
Maloney, George, *The Spirit Broods Over the World* (Alba House 1993)
O'Connor, Edward, *Pope Paul and the Spirit* (Ave Maria Press 1978)
Ramsey, Michael, *Holy Spirit* (SPCK 1977)

CHAPTER SEVEN

THE HOLY CATHOLIC CHURCH

THE CHURCH AS A MYSTERY OF FAITH

(CATECHISM, 770-776)

The starting point of *Lumen Gentium* represented nothing less than a Copernican revolution in our understanding of the Church. Decisively rejected was a preoccupation with the institutional aspect of the Church which, when carried to extremes, was understood simply in terms of the Pope and the authority of the Church of Rome. Instead, priority was now given to what is most important about the Church: the special presence within it of the mystery of God who calls all peoples to himself and sustains them in his love. The words of Jesus to his disciples are equally applicable to the Church of today: 'To you has been given the secret (*mysterion*) of the kingdom of God' (Mark 4:11). He was telling them of the mystery of God's love which had been hidden for endless ages, which had been for centuries the foundation of Jewish hope, and which was now being made known to them in his person.

St Paul expresses the full extent of this mystery when he writes: 'He has let us know the mystery of his purpose, according to his good pleasure which he determined beforehand in Christ, for him to act upon when the times had run their course: that he would bring everything together under Christ, as head, everything in the heavens and everything on earth' (Ephesians 1:9). The Church, therefore, has always at its heart something mysterious because it shares ultimately in the mysterious life of God. The Church's secret is God's secret: 'Something which has existed since the beginning, which we have heard, which we have seen with our own eyes; which we have watched and touched with our own hands: the Word of life – this is our theme' (1 John 1:1-4).

The secret of Jesus in his relationship with the Father has been made totally available to us within the Church: 'As the Father has loved me so I have loved you.'

Every aspect of the Church's life, therefore, must remain rooted in an awareness of the mystery of God, a mystery which is impossible to comprehend and yet to which we are commissioned to bear witness. Just a number of consequences can be mentioned:

> We can never fully grasp the mystery of God, the greater part of which lies in darkness, beyond our reach; indeed the more we discover about God, the greater becomes the presence of his mystery and love; we can never say the final word about God, there is always more to share, there is always more to experience; and therefore the mystery of God invites us 'to listen as well as to teach, to be humble and searching as well as being guide and beacon'.[1]

> No longer can we look upon the Church as the exclusive community of those who are saved; mystery cannot so easily be confined. Rather, the Church is the sacrament of the world's salvation, a sign of that Word from God which says that God loves the world, that God is met in life, and that our future belongs to God. The Church names the mystery which permeates life wherever it is to be found and which will be fully revealed in the fulness of time. In the words of Gaudium et Spes: 'It is the Church's task to uncover, cherish, and enoble all that is true, good and beautiful in the human community'.[2]

> Finally, we cannot define the Church; we can only understand the Church indirectly: in symbols, in images, in metaphors, in all those forms of language which point to her essential mystery rather than define her. If we take any one image and feel that we have

pinned her down, we have lost her. She escapes all definition. In the scriptures, therefore, images are taken 'from the life of a shepherd, or from cultivation of the land, from the art of building or from family life and marriage' (Lumen Gentium 6). The Catechism lists a number of such images as follows: a sheepfold, a vineyard, a building, and a bride (pars. 754-757). But the principal images are those of the Church as the People of God and the Body of Christ.

THE CHURCH AS THE PEOPLE OF GOD

(CATECHISM 781-786)

The principal model of the Church in the documents of Vatican II is that of the People of God. It is a biblical concept which has deep roots in the Old Testament where Israel is frequently referred to as a People formed by God (Exodus 19:4-6). He is their God and they are his people, and He will never fail them. Apart from their relationship to God they are 'No people', a lost people without hope and without life. Even though they were the 'least of all peoples', he chose them to be the bearer of his promises. In several New Testament texts, the Christian Church is referred to as the new Israel or as the People of God of the new Covenant (cf 1 Peter 2:9).

In *Lumen Gentium*, the chapter on 'The People of God' precedes the chapter on 'The Hierarchical Structure of the Church'. This way of ordering the two chapters was the result of protracted debate and it has profound consequences for our understanding of the Church.

Church and Israel (Catechism pars. 839-840)

The notion of the Church as the People of God is a powerful symbol expressing the continuity of the Church with Israel. There has been a story of two thousand years of misunderstanding and persecution, of defamation and distrust, of ignorance and prejudice, reaching a devastating climax in the 'Holocaust' of the Third Reich. Less than a hundred years ago, at the First Vatican Council, a document had been prepared which asked Jews to give up their 'futile' waiting for a Messiah and to acknowledge Christ. It is fortunate, in this respect, that war brought a speedy end to the Council's deliberations.

After a long and stormy passage, the Second Vatican Council's declaration on non-Christian religions rejected in no uncertain terms the charge that the Jews were guilty of 'deicide' and urged Christians to recognise the fundamental unity of Jewish and Christian faith. As Christians, we are called upon to recognise our spiritual origin from Israel, as we both appeal to one and the same God. The Jews are and remain God's chosen and beloved people; the Jews remain the people God addressed first. We must remember, too, that Jesus was a Jew, a fact which gives urgency to his prayer: 'May they be one', an appeal for unity and love among Jews and non-Jews in the one People of God.

Furthermore, the continuing Jewish witness forces Christianity at all times to face the fact that it has not arrived at its goal, has not arrived at the fullness of truth, but is always a wayfarer waiting in hope. In the words of Martin Buber: 'The expectation of Christians is directed towards the Second Coming, that of the Jews to a Coming that has not been anticipated by a first. But both can wait for the advent of the One together, and there are moments when they may prepare the way before him together.' Within the one People of God, therefore, the name 'Jew' is never an insult but the honourable name of the people who are the bearer of God's promises. (cf recent guidelines on Christian/Jewish relationships published by the Bishops of England and Wales).

Called by God (Catechism pars. 542-543)

Fundamental to the experience of being the People of God is the notion of election and call: 'For you are a people consecrated to Yahweh your God; of all the peoples on earth, you have been chosen by Yahweh your God to be his own people. Yahweh set his heart on you and chose you not because you were the most numerous of all peoples . . . but because he loved you' (Deuteronomy 7:6-7). This means that there should be no second-class citizens within the fellowship of Christians. All have equal rights and obligations, even though their capacities, desires or abilities to exercise them may differ widely. All share in the one Spirit. Centuries ago Jeremiah proclaimed the words of Yahweh in the following terms:

> 'Within them I shall plant my Law, writing it on their hearts. Then I shall be their God and they shall be my people. There will be no further need for everyone to teach neighbour or brother, saying "Learn to know Yahweh!" No, they will all know me, from the least to the greatest, Yahweh declares, since I shall forgive their guilt and never more call their sin to mind.'
> (Jeremiah 31:33-34)

This prophecy finds fulfilment in the New Testament which describes the presence of the Spirit of Christ within all as an inner illumination:

> 'It is God who said, "Let light shine out of darkness", that has shone into our hearts to enlighten them with the knowledge of God's glory, the glory on the face of Christ.'
> (2 Corinthians 4:6)

In addition to our basic equality within the People of God, the notion of election brings home to us the passion of God for his people. Our God is no cold, silent, heavenly power who sits self-sufficiently upon his throne. He displays a great passion for creation, for human beings, for whom his love is particular, personal and for everybody. When one considers, however, the numbers of people that have populated our world and continue to do so, then this supreme mystery of our faith can seem so unreal. And yet, we know in faith that we are called, we are loved. We know in faith that 'Christ loves me', that 'Christ died for me'. We know that God reaches out to the ends of the earth to seek out and save what was lost; that not a hair falls out of our heads without our heavenly Father noticing. Life, wherever it is to be found, has been passionately confirmed and accepted by God in Jesus Christ.

A Pilgrim People (Catechism par. 769)

Our being the People of God brings home to us that we are essentially a pilgrim people. Such an understanding recalls one of the basic themes of the bible: from the call to Abraham to leave his own country and to travel to an unknown land, to Israel's wanderings in the desert, to Christ's own journey to Jerusalem, and to the pilgrim Church which carries the mark of this world 'until there be realised new heavens and a new earth in which justice dwells.'[4] This image of being on a journey carries with it a number of important implications:

> Within the Church we are all on a journey to God and not everyone is at the same point in the journey. We have experienced different stories of faith; we have received various kinds of support and encouragement. All of this must be taken into account as we reflect upon how we must relate to each other and, indeed, to ourselves. We have to learn to live with people whose understanding of the faith may be very different from our own; we have to be ready to listen to and learn from each other, respecting each other's experience of God; and we have to grow in knowledge and self-realisation, ever struggling to discover God in the depths of our own life and of the lives of everyone.

A pilgrim church is a church for the sinner, which means that the Church is for all. 'If we say that we share in God's life while we are living in darkness, we are lying, because we are not living the truth' (1 John 1:8). Many experience this aspect of the Church as a serious obstacle to faith, and, of course, it is if accompanied by a terrible blindness which breeds self-righteousness and lack of compassion. But if the Church's sinfulness is truly acknowledged then it results in a tremendous openness of heart both to Jesus as Saviour and to those who stand in need of his healing love. We experience the true God who is our Father and in whom there is no condemnation. He does not judge, he does not punish, he does not retaliate; He only forgives. Our sin may be great but God's love is always the greater. It is only out of the experience of such need for forgiveness and of being forgiven that the Church is able to reach out into people's lives supporting them in their weakness. The Church, therefore, does not merely tolerate sinners at the periphery; this 'Church embraces sinners in its very bosom'.⁵ (cf Catechism par. 827).

Finally, a pilgrim church is called to enduring hope; this is so vital in a world which speaks so frequently of the absence of God and where people have been hurt too much and too often and have too little cause for rejoicing. Life can seem so pointless: men and women disabled, God remote and unconcerned. Job speaks for so many when he says: 'Remember that my life is but a breath, and that my eyes will never again see joy' (Job 7:7). We need to be a people in whom attitudes of fear, suspicion, self-interest and anxiety are largely replaced by joy, hope, trust, openness, love and peace. We need to have confidence in the words of Jesus: 'Do not let your hearts be troubled. Trust in God still, and trust in me' (John 14:1).

THE CHURCH AS THE BODY OF CHRIST

(CATECHISM PARS. 787-796)

The Church's true distinctiveness, however, lies in her relationship with the Lord Jesus. *Lumen Gentium*, therefore, draws out the significance of that marvellous text in St John's Gospel which speaks of the blood and water flowing from the open side of the crucified Jesus (cf John 19:34), and which is foretold in the words of the Lord referring to his death on the cross: 'And when I am lifted up from the earth, I shall draw all people to myself' (John 12:32).[6]

For St Paul, too, we are so inseparable from the resurrection itself that he can only speak of us as the body of Christ. This lay at the heart of his Damascus experience: 'Saul, Saul, why are you persecuting me?' (Acts 9:4) – an experience which preoccupies St Paul throughout all his writings. To the embarrassment of a later age, he expresses our communion with Christ in the most physical terms: 'Do you not realise that anyone who attaches himself to a prostitute is one body with her, since the two, as it is said, become one flesh. But anyone who attaches himself to the Lord is one spirit with him' (1 Corinthians 6:17).

As risen Lord, therefore, Jesus is present to us now much more intimately than he could have been before his passion and death. He can now enter our inmost being, fill us with his peace, unite us ever more closely to his own life and become personally present to us in a way no one else can. In the words of St Paul: 'I have been crucified with Christ, and yet I am alive; yet it is no longer I, but Christ living in me' (Galatians 2:20). Such an intimate relationship to the Lord Jesus gives rise to a number of important considerations:

The Church as Communion

The basic model for our understanding of the church is that of 'Communion'. With the current breakdown of community life, and people desperately seeking mutual support in all kinds of ways, it is most important that the church encourages ways of drawing people into an experience of their common life in Christ. It is in him that our relationship with God is defined. He is God with us, taking away our sense of isolation and alienation. The message of Jesus is essentially a call to conversion and communion with God: 'I have loved you just as the Father has loved me. Remain in my love . . . This is my commandment: love one another as I have loved you' (John 15:9,12; 1 John 1:3-4).

Such an ideal is clearly put before us by the church of the Acts of the Apostles: 'And all who shared the faith owned everything in common; they sold their goods and possessions and distributed the proceeds among themselves according to what each one needed' (Acts 2:44-45). And, we are told, 'The whole group of believers was united, heart and soul; no one claimed private ownership of any possessions, as everything they owned was held in common' (Acts 4:32). Such is the vision that must be held out for us by the Church: God has made us to live in communion with one another. God has not made us as isolated individuals who do not need one another, who can stand alone in splendid isolation. God has made us for one another.

The Church as Local Church (Catechism pars. 832-833)

Such communion is experienced, first and foremost, within the local church. This is the church which is within our range, our experience, within our grasp. It is here that Christ is present, in the Gospel read and expounded, in the Eucharist which is shared, and in the love which results from both. And so, in *Lumen Gentium*, we read: 'The Church of Christ is truly present in all legitimate local congregations of the faithful which, united with their bishops, are themselves called Churches in the New Testament.'[7] Starting with the local church is important for a number of reasons, two of the basic ones being as follows:

> First of all, it is *scriptural:* the Acts of the Apostles speaks regularly of 'the church in Jerusalem' (Acts 5:11; 8:1); and then, as Christianity spread outwards from

Jerusalem, of each of the various communities, as is instanced particularly at the beginning of Paul's letters: 'the church of God which is in Corinth' (1 Corinthians 1:2; 2 Corinthians 1:1). It is to this community, too, that Paul addresses the following words: 'The blessing-cup which we bless, is it not a sharing in the blood of Christ; and the loaf of bread which we break, is it not a sharing in the body of Christ? And as there is one loaf, so we, although there are many of us, are one single body, for we all share in the one loaf' (1 Corinthians 10: 16-17). The Eucharist can only be celebrated somewhere, at a particular time. The Church of Christ is present in all its mystery and reality in the local church; the local church is where the Church happens.

Secondly, it draws attention to that vital ingredient of *diversity* within the Church. We are now more conscious of the Church as a communion of local churches giving expression to the diversity and universality of the people of God. Such diversity is expressed by Vatican II in a most positive way in the following terms: 'The variety of local churches living with one another in harmony is particularly splendid evidence of the catholicity of the undivided Church.'[8] This is true not only of the variety of churches within our own neighbourhood and even within our own country, but also of the Church on the world stage as well. We are now beginning to experience the Church as a world-Church, especially with the emergence of the churches in Africa, Asia and Latin America. Just as Jesus lived and died in the flesh and blood of his own people, so is the Church gradually being rooted in each culture. The special characteristics of a people, the varied gifts of the Spirit, are finding visible expression in the life and culture of local churches (Catechism par. 814).

A Church of Hospitality and Welcome

Finally, as Christians in communion, we are called first and foremost to be a place of welcome where we are able to recognise that God is our Father whose love embraces us in every moment of the day. We are called to create a sense of belonging in our local churches for newcomers, single people, single parent families, the divorced and remarried, the unemployed, the sick, the disabled, the housebound, the elderly, the poor – indeed, for all those whom Jesus calls his own. Being in communion means a new way of living together which says that no one is alone with his or her disabilities; we are all, without exception, called to be part of the one body of Christ. Perhaps, in our own time, special attention needs to be given to the following:

> The need to respond warmly to the many demands made upon the Church to be present at moments of birth and death. Though many may not be practising, they still have faith and turn to the Church to make sense of their lives, especially in those critical moments, which are caught up in the mystery of God.

> The need to help young people to feel at home within the Church. This constitutes a great challenge for us all: how can we overcome a sense of alienation which is felt by so many of our young people today and which is causing so much heartache to their parents? What are they seeking? What are they rejecting? In the words of Pope Paul VI: how can we offer them the gospel ideal as something to be known and lived?[9]

> The need to listen to the experience of women within the Church, both married and single. Times have changed since St Teresa of Avila made the comment: 'We poor women are not wanted anywhere!' But much still needs to be done if we are to take seriously the recent report *Do Not Be Afraid:* 'There is greater

sharing across gender in the fields of employment, family life, and leisure. The result is that the apparent discrimination which is practised in the Church is becoming increasingly obvious and difficult to reconcile with women's lived experience, especially for younger women.'[10] In the recent Synod, too, (October 1994), there were assertions from all quarters that women should be given a greater role in the Church.

The need for support when a marriage fails: 'We must reach out with love – the love of Christ – to those who know the pain of failure in marriage; to those who know the loneliness of bringing up a family on their own . . . I praise all those who help people wounded by the breakdown of their marriage, by showing them Christ's compassion and counselling them according to Christ's truth.'[11]

The need to respect the human and religious rights of 'non-Catholic' partners in mixed marriages and to encourage particular pastoral care of such couples in our parishes. Once again, Pope John Paul II has spoken of such marriages in the most positive terms: 'You live in your marriage the hopes and difficulties of the path to Christian unity. Express that hope in prayer together, in the unity of love.' (York 1982).

HOLY, CATHOLIC CHURCH

In the words of 'The Easter People', the Bishops' response to the National Pastoral Congress of 1980:

'The Church is in the world and exists for the world. Like Jesus Christ her Lord, she must constantly place herself at the service of her fellow-men, recognising the vital part she has to play in this life, humanising and developing the world here and now, making it a more human place, and if more human, then more divine, because we are made in the image of God.'[12]

The Creed speaks of this mission in terms of the Church being one, holy, catholic and apostolic – traditionally referred to as marks of the Church. These marks of the Church, identifying the Church as Christ's Church, are not only gifts, granted to the Church by the grace of God, but at the same time demands which are placed upon the Church if it is to be true to its mission. The marks of the Church must become the marks of Christian people. We shall now consider those marks which are referred to in the Apostles Creed: the Holy, Catholic Church.

The Church is Holy (Catechism 823-829)

Only God, properly speaking, can be called holy; it speaks of his otherness, his awe-inspiring majesty: 'Holy, holy, holy is Yahweh Sabaoth. His glory fills the whole earth' (Isaiah 6:3). This theme is central to the preaching of Isaiah, who frequently speaks of Yahweh as 'the Holy One of Israel' (1:4; 5:19; 10:17). But perhaps the most dramatic experience of the holiness of God belongs to Moses when God called to him from the middle of the burning bush: '"Moses, Moses!" he said. "Here I am" he answered. "Come no nearer", he said. "Take off your sandals, for the place where you are standing is holy ground. I am the God of your ancestors . . ."' (Exodus 3:1-6).

In the person of Jesus, and through the power of the Spirit, 'the Holy One of Israel' has come close, and has transformed creation and all within it by his presence. No longer is the holiness of God to be associated simply with special places and particular groups of people. In Christ all the baptised are called to be living temples of the Spirit, dwelling places for God. We are called to be 'a chosen race, a kingdom of priests, a holy nation, a people to be a personal possession to sing the praises of God who called you out of the darkness into the wonderful light' (1 Peter 2:9).

This universal call to holiness carries a number of important implications for our appreciation of the Church and its mission:

> In acknowledging the Church as 'holy', we must resist the temptation to exclude the 'sinful' members from the Church so that only the spiritual elite, the sinless, the pure, the holy are left. Such religious separatism was something Jesus refused to advocate, making it his business to seek out and save the lost (Matthew 13:24-30). In opposition to the Pharisees, 'the separated ones', Jesus knew that all communities are a mixture of the good and the bad. And it is not always easy to tell which is which! The same attitude must prevail within the Church – a church of saints and sinners – on the way to holiness and so always in need of penance and renewal. The salutary advice of St Paul must always be remembered: 'Do not judge anything before the due time, until the Lord comes' (1 Corinthians 4:5).

> In the words of St Paul again, 'we are all called to take our place amongst the saints' (1 Corinthians 1:2). There are no privileged, higher states of life within the Church; there is no vocation which is holier than any other. In the past it has often been assumed that bishops, priests, and religious are the only ones who are really called to a life of holiness; the lay people were more or less encouraged to tag along. Such an assumption runs counter, of course, to the summons of Jesus which calls all of us to 'be perfect just as (our) heavenly Father is perfect' (Matthew 5:48). Whatever our service or ministry within the Church, God lives within each of us; we not only *can* be holy, we *are* holy.

> All of us are called to holiness but in different ways. An essential task of the ordained ministry, for example, is to enable the many varied gifts of the Spirit to flourish

within the community and so build up the body of Christ. It is a matter of helping people to realise their true calling as bearers of Christ for one another. Lay people, on the other hand, are called to holiness principally through the circumstances of their ordinary everyday lives. Every parent who has suffered sleepless nights with a wakeful child, every person caring for someone who is elderly or sick, every extra effort to attend to the needs of strangers or the life of the community – there is an event of grace, the closeness of God. In and through the many varied experiences of life they are called upon to name and celebrate what is sacred, what is holy.

The Church is Catholic (Catechism 830-856)

The term 'catholic' means whole and universal. The earliest known use of the term in connection with the Church is found in the letter of St Ignatius of Antioch to the church of Smyrna: 'Wherever the bishop appears, there is the community, just as where Jesus Christ is, there is the catholic Church.' It is most probable that St Ignatius is distinguishing between the local eucharistic assembly and the Church 'as a whole', in its entirety. By the fourth century, however, when the word first appeared in the Western creeds, 'catholicity' came to be recognised as a mark of the true Church, and so 'catholic' came to mean the opposite of heretical. Both these meanings of 'catholicity' are connected:

• Catholicity and the local church (Catechism 832-835)

As we have seen, the local church is nothing less than the Church of Christ in a particular place. But, in identifying the Church with a particular locality, there is a danger of the local church becoming a separated unity giving rise to narrowness and sectarian attitudes. And so, within the local church, there must be a consciousness of belonging to the universal Church, a sense of catholicity. This is vital if individual churches, and individuals too, are not to live a monadic existence, private and autonomous, but are to live in communion with one another, encouraging and challenging each other in love and with mutual concern for true peace and justice. As Yves Congar has written: 'The Christian experience within the local community is that of the unity of the whole People of God'.[13]

• *Catholicity as unity in diversity*

Understanding the Church in this way, as a communion of local churches, means that 'catholicity' is contrasted with mere 'uniformity'. What makes the unity of the Church 'catholic' is the rich variety of races and cultures that make up the one Church of Christ. In the words of Vatican II: 'The variety of local churches with one common aspiration is particularly splendid evidence of the catholicity of the undivided Church' (Lumen Gentium 23). And again: '. . . it has come about that various churches established in diverse places by the apostles and their successors . . . pre-serving the unity of faith. . . enjoy their own discipline, their own liturgical usage, and their own theological and spiritual heritage'.[14]

• *Catholicity and Christian unity*

This same diversity must extend to our understanding of the kind of unity we seek with other Christian churches. It cannot mean 'surrender' to Roman Catholicism; nor can it mean the creation of a single, united Church in which all diversity is played down. Rather, the unity we seek and pray for will be far richer when it gathers up 'all the diversities of traditions and individuals, all the riches that have been unpacked and developed throughout the Church's pilgrimage'.[15] The principle of catholicity demands that the goal of the ecumenical movement must be a form of unity 'in which there will be a large variety of languages, of ritual forms, of historical traditions, of local prerogatives, of spiritual currents, of legitimate institutions and preferred activities'.[16]

• *Catholicity as responsibility of the bishops*

Establishing catholicity within the Church is a major responsibility for our diocesan bishops. They must ensure this openness within the local churches, this communion with the universal Church, through their communion with their fellow bishops, and most particularly with the Bishop of Rome. It did not take long for the Church to recognise the need, in case of doubt, for a criterion to judge whether a particular bishop was in communion or not. In the beginning, such a criterion would be based on agreement with many other bishops. A more stable criterion, however, was agreement with the apostolic sees, that is, those sees where the apostles had once worked, or which had received apostolic letters. These were the centres of apostolic witness with which all other sees had to align themselves. Whoever was in communion with them was in the Catholic Church.

Within this context, Rome held a particularly prominent position because it could claim three apostles as its own – Peter, Paul and John. By the third century, Rome alone is looked upon as 'the apostolic see – the final proper and self-sufficient criterion of catholicity'. And so we read in *Lumen Gentium*: 'Each individual bishop represents his own church, but all of them together in union with the Pope represent the entire Church joined in the bond of peace, love, and unity.'[17]

Such harmony, however, is not always possible. There is conflict and disagreement between local churches, including the Church of Rome. It is never easy to do justice to local pastoral needs within the wider context of the Catholic communion as a whole. That is why catholicity is not simply a gift but a challenge. It can help us to realise that disagreement and tension, far from being destructive, may be creative moments in the growth towards full communion.

NOTES

1 Cardinal Hume, *The Times* October 11th, 1977
2 Vatican II: *Gaudium et Spes*, no. 76
3 Martin Buber, *Israel and the World* (1948) p. 39
4 Vatican II, *Lumen Gentium*, no. 48
5 Vatican II: *Lumen Gentium*, no. 8
6 Vatican II: *Lumen Gentium*, no. 7
7 Vatican II: *Lumen Gentium*, no. 26
8 Vatican II: *Decree on Eastern Churches*, pars. 2-3
9 Pope Paul VI: *On Evangelisation* (1975), no. 72
10 *'Do Not Be Afraid'* (Redemptorist Publications 1992) p. 37
11 *The Pope in Britain* (St Paul Publications 1982)
12 *The Easter People in Liverpool* (1980), p. 372
13 Yves Congar, *Power and Poverty,* p. 6
14 Vatican II: *Lumen Gentium*, 23
15 John McQuarrie, *Christian Unity and Diversity* (SCM 1974), p. 3
16 Pope Paul VI, *Evangelii Nuntiandi* (1975), no. 64
17 Vatican II: *Lumen Gentium*, par. 23

FURTHER READING

Catechism of the Catholic Church: pars. 748-943
Dulles, Avery, *Models of the Church* (Gill & MacMillan 1974)
Kung, Hans, *The Church* (Burns & Oates, 1967)
Kress, Robert, *The Church, Communion, Sacrament, Communication* (Paulist Press 1985)
Lavery, Hugh, *Reflections on the Creed* (St Paul Publications 1982)
Sullivan, Francis, *The Church We Believe In* (Gill & MacMillan 1988)

CHAPTER EIGHT

WE LOOK FOR THE RESURRECTION
OF THE DEAD
AND LIFE EVERLASTING

DEATH IS MYSTERIOUS AND THREATENING

Every day countless numbers of people die, thousands upon thousands and millions upon millions. Death is the most familiar of human phenomena, as common as salt. And yet, despite its being so commonplace, there is no death like my death. Each of us, without exception, must face up to death and it is only natural that we should be afraid.

The Fear of Dying

We are afraid of the unknown, afraid of the dark, a terrifying darkness in which we might simply cease to be; we are afraid of falling apart, of losing our dignity in our dying, of losing contact with those closest to us; we are afraid of pain and the implications of our medical condition. St Therese of Lisieux, despite her overwhelming desire of God, experienced doubts, anxiety, a fear of death, a dark night of the soul, when she could not pray or bring herself to believe in eternal life: 'If you only knew the darkness'.[1] Such feelings are understandable when death seems to confront us with total impossibility. How can there be any future for this person who has ceased to be? How can these dry bones live? Death would seem to be blank horror, unspeakable tragedy, without any savour of hope, the final victory of sin over us (cf Catechism par. 1006-1007).

A Fear of Hell

In addition to the natural fears surrounding death and the pain of dying, many Christians experience a fear of everlasting hell. Their faith, far from helping them in the face of death, has frequently served to intensify their anxiety by overwhelming them with a sense of guilt. Many of us are familiar with those powerful retreat sermons which described in such vivid detail the unbearable physical torments of a hell which lasted for ever and ever. They presented God as a stern and stony God of endless demand and infinite reprisal, a God who condemns for repeated failure. Far from rejoicing in the thought of being united with the risen Lord, many a Christian has been utterly depressed by the thought of approaching death.[2]

There are a number of reasons, therefore, why we should be afraid of death. But it is unnatural when something as normal and as inevitable as death becomes a terror for us, when it diminishes our living, and becomes a source of morbid preoccupation. We need to reflect upon differing attitudes towards death.

CHANGING ATTITUDES TO DEATH

A Familiar Experience

In days gone by, death was very much a family affair. Many children died young, the elderly died where they had lived within the family home, surrounded by those closest to them. Solzhenitsyn, in Cancer Ward, describes this attitude well when he writes:

> 'The old folk didn't puff themselves up or fight against it or brag that they weren't going to die – they took death calmly. They did not shirk squaring things up, they prepared themselves

quietly and in good time, deciding who should
have the mare, who the coat and who the boots.
And they departed easily, as if they were just
moving into a new house."

An ideal picture, certainly, but it does indicate the way in
which people, throughout their lives, were very close to the
experience of death.

A Gradual Distancing from Death

• Isolation of the family unit

Such a romantic picture of death, as described above, has
changed dramatically. People have, in fact, become unfamiliar
with the experience of death. We no longer live in villages or
in close-knit parishes where relatives and friends
spontaneously gather round their loved ones who are dying.
Such occasions are rare. People die in hospitals, suddenly in
accidents, or alone in their bed-sitters. A recent survey has
shown that seventy-four per cent of people who die in hospital
die alone without their family and friends to support them.

• Advance in technology

People today expect to live their full span of life. Vast
improvements have been made in the whole area of hygiene
and we have witnessed remarkable developments in the field
of medical science: in natal care, in intensive care units, in the
increasing availability of drugs, organ transplants and life
support systems. It would seem that the possibilities of
continuing to live are endless. It is not surprising that the
doctor who is justifiably committed to the fullest potential of
life wherever possible should almost feel cheated when his
efforts fail.

• Evasion of death

We are familiar with the modern preoccupation with keeping
young and healthy by visiting health farms, by undergoing
cosmetic surgery, by slimming and dieting. Much of it, of

course, is good and to be recommended; but much of it, too, suggests trying to escape the inevitable onset of mortality. It would seem that we wish to keep all thought of death stubbornly at bay, hoping against hope for a last minute antidote. No wonder our culture has been described as a death-denying culture.

A New Awareness of Death

The Scale of Death

Today we are overwhelmed by the sheer scale of death, death brought about by human intent and on a massive scale. Millions of people have been killed in wars and revolutions, in prisons and concentration camps; millions of others have died in the Third World from malnutrition and abject poverty. Yet the magnitude of this death is rendered miniscule by the possibilities of the unspeakable horror of a nuclear holocaust – still a threat despite the ending of the Cold War. In the first few moments of a nuclear exchange hundreds of millions of people would lose their lives. In the words of Cardinal Hume: 'Our age stands self-condemned for having invented so horrendous a weapon, and for having spent so much on it.'

Medical Advance

The remarkable developments in the field of medical science, already referred to, have themselves generated a great interest in medico-ethical problems relating to death. We are familiar with the issues of abortion and euthanasia, but with the development of organ transplants it has become vitally important to know when death occurs and what tests are available for discerning the moment of death. The increase in life-support systems, too, has given rise more than ever to the terrible dilemma of whether 'to save or let die', which has become a major preoccupation involving doctors, nurses, social workers, lawyers and the general public.

Care for the Dying

Of particular importance, is the growing realisation that the dying, just as much as anyone else if not more so, need skilled medical and nursing care. Three women, in recent times, have made a tremendous impact in this connection: Mother Teresa, Dame Cicely Saunders, and Elizabeth Kubler Ross.

Mother Teresa is known the world over for her work amongst the poor of Calcutta, helping them to die with dignity: 'I spend hours and hours in serving the sick, and the dying, the unwanted, the unloved, the lepers, the mentally ill – because I love God and I believe his word: "You did it to me".' In her experience, many die a beautiful death, loved and cared for and in peace with God.

Dame Cicely Saunders is well known as the pioneer of the hospice movement. The Founder and Director of the famous St Christopher's Hospice in London, she is referred to as 'the woman who has changed the face of death'. She places emphasis upon total care both for the dying and their families. Particular attention is given to the control of pain and the distressing symptoms which are often associated with terminal illness. Her whole approach is one of esteem, reverence and loving kindness.

Elizabeth Kubler Ross, finally, has done so much to liberate people from the fears of dying by stressing the need to create an atmosphere of trust and openness. She has spoken of the dying as our teachers and, by patiently listening to them, she has helped us to understand the basic emotions involved in coming to terms with personal death.

SPEAKING ABOUT DEATH AND BEYOND

Temptation towards Literal Description

Many of us have felt the temptation to try to speak 'exactly' about death, and even about whatever lies beyond death. We need only reflect upon the kind of curiosity which finds expression in crudely literal questions about heaven and hell.

Inevitably, the language of fire and burning and physical pain, all too familiar in human experience, is much more meaningful than the far more elusive and ethereal language of the beatific vision. It is easier to describe a convincing hell than a convincing heaven. Unfortunately, this has had the effect of focussing people's attention not on the content of Christian hope but rather on its deprivation.

We must resist the temptation of this way of speaking because we have no experience, our own or anyone else's, of what lies beyond death. There have been attempts to peep beyond the darkness of death through the testimony of those who have been 'clinically dead'. But they can only speak of the experience that leads up to death and nothing more. There is no information about the 'next' world. The new life beyond death remains something for which we can hope, but which is beyond our vision or imagination.

Use of Poetry, Metaphor, Symbol

We must learn to live with the fact that the only available language in which we can speak about the mystery of death and beyond is the language of poetry, metaphor and symbol. In this whole matter, language reaches its limits. The mystery of God will always remain ineffable and any attempt to elaborate Christian hope is bound to be totally inadequate. God's reality lies beyond our vision; his prodigal love is too great for the human heart to grasp. In the words of St Paul: 'It is as Scripture says: "What no eye has seen and no ear has heard, what the mind of man cannot visualise; all that God has prepared for those who love him"' (1 Corinthians 2:9).

Need for Precision

It is not a matter of indifference, however, which symbols and images are used to express our faith in Christian hope. This is why the Church over the centuries has sought 'to guard against error' in a matter in which we can only use metaphor and symbol:

At stake in the Church's teaching on hell and individual judgement is the fact that death is final and that we are ultimately accountable for what we do with our lives. There is no process of human maturing after death. We must respond to the challenge of growing in the image and likeness of God in the course of our biological life here on earth or not at all (cf Catechism pars. 1013-1014).

Equally important is the Church's insistence on resurrection of the body. St Paul rightly warns us against asking stupid questions about the kind of body we shall receive (1 Corinthians 15:35ff), but to express Christian hope in bodily terms is to imply something about the way our present life is to be evaluated. It implies that the social dimensions of our lives have ultimate importance. It means that any notion of heaven and hell or kingdom of God cannot imply a devaluation of concern for the present world. Without the preaching of justice there is no Gospel of Jesus Christ. At all times, our task as Christians is to protest against injustice, to challenge what is un-human, and to side with the poor and the oppressed (Matthew 25; Luke 4:18; cf Catechism pars. 999-1000)

Despite the limitations of human language, therefore, we must speak of the mystery of death and seek to do justice to that hope which lies within the human heart.

DEATH ENGAGES THE WHOLE PERSON

Death as Separation of Soul and Body

We are reminded, once again, of that familiar catechism question: 'Of which must I take most care, of my body or of my soul?' Perhaps it was the wrong question but it does indicate a bias within much of Christian tradition which has shaped our perception of death. Is it not true that death is still commonly perceived as a separation of the soul from the body? While the body is placed in the coffin and subsequently disintegrates in the grave, the soul arrives before the judgement seat of God where its eternal destiny is decided. In a way, death is looked upon as the great liberator, coming to free in us that which is truly human – the soul or spirit – while the body is destroyed. Christian hope is thereby conceived in terms of being 'freed from the body'.

It is now recognised that a number of serious difficulties accompany such an understanding:

> It encourages a preoccupation with the next life and a lack of concern for the present one. If our real treasure is in another world, we can easily become indifferent to the injustices of this world.

> Stress upon the 'immortality of the soul' seems to suggest that we possess an 'indestructible bit' that doesn't die. But, as we shall see, death involves the whole person – both body and soul die and both rise to newness of life.[4]

Unity of the Human Person

We must take seriously the unity of the human person. The physical and spiritual aspects of our lives interrelate so closely and overlap so extensively that the only valid viewpoint is an holistic one. The spiritual and physical aspects can be distinguished but never separated. We are aware of our capacity to know and love and we realise that there never is a time when we can love another completely. There is always an element of the other which is always inaccessible, always beyond the grasp of our love. But this capacity to know and love, activities which belong properly to the soul, is not a detachable part of our human nature, capable of independent activity and existence. On the contrary, we know from human experience that the body is the only means whereby we can communicate. We cannot see inside another person directly;

we can only grasp their spirit, the power that drives them on, through the rich vocabulary of word and gesture. We never see courage directly, we only see courageous actions; we never see despair directly, we only see despair through sad eyes, through an inability to act, through a paralysing inertia; and we never see love directly but through loving words and actions. Far from being a barrier, our body is our only life-line to the rest of creation and to God.

Resurrection of the Body

We are only too well aware that our experience of relationship and communication with others is far from strong. We suffer from incompleteness, from fear and uncertainty, from an inability to communicate, and from that dehumanising force within us that we call sin. In biblical terms, we are people of the flesh, weak, vulnerable, perishable and powerless. We are called to be people of the spirit, filled with the power and dynamism of God. That is why it is the whole person that dies – body and soul – and by the power of God is brought into the fullness of life. Faith in the resurrection is the humanising force in us, enabling us to break free of the limitations of weakness and sinfulness, so that we become transformed by and penetrated with the spirit of the risen Christ. In that transformation we shall become fully human.

This means that our personal resurrection is only the initial thrust of our future life. Personal resurrection hungers for the resurrection of all people into that fullness of life with God. Those who have died and gone before us in faith will not enjoy complete freedom until the transformation of the world has come to pass. No one is fully alive while others die. And so, not only is St Therese of Lisieux spending her heaven doing good on earth, but all the faithful departed are actively awaiting that Day when our God will be all in all.

In the immortal lines of John Donne: 'No man is an island, entire of itself. Any man's death diminishes me because I am involved in mankind. And therefore never send to know for whom the bell tolls. It tolls for thee'. In a passage of great beauty,

Donne expresses the profound unity at the heart of humankind. This means that our body is not self enclosed, an isolated entity, but includes everyone and everything that has made us the people we are. Our language, our families, our towns and cities, are part of us. We are inevitably reminded of passages from St Paul who frequently employs the metaphor of body and sees the Church, humankind, indeed the whole of creation, in the process of being reborn and made one: 'All of us, in union with Christ, form one body, and as parts of it we belong to each other' (Romans 12:5). And again: 'From the beginning till now the entire creation, as we know, has been groaning in one great act of giving birth' (Romans 8:22). As Donne reminds us, therefore, when we die we never die alone; the whole network of personal, family and social communications of which we formed a part, die a little too. 'Any man's death diminishes me because I am involved in mankind.'

Such an understanding of the wider reference of the human body can only enrich our appreciation of the resurrection of the body. It means that not only our naked self is saved through death but that our whole life history and the memories and relationships that have shaped our history are brought to their final consummation. In the words of a recent theologian:

> 'God loves more than the molecules that happen to be in the body at the time of death . . . the Resurrection of the body means that . . . all the tears have been gathered and no smile has been allowed to slip away unnoticed. Resurrection of the body means that we find in God not only our last moments, but our whole story. It is not for nothing that . . . the Risen Christ is said to bear the marks of his wounds.'
> Wilhelm Breuning, Concilium, 1968, p. 9

Dying, therefore, is not something that takes place just in our last few weeks or hours. It does not succeed life; it belongs to the whole process of living.[5]

Experience of Living as a School for Dying

Natural Rhythms of Life

Life itself is a process of striving for growth; we need to die in order to live. It is simply the basic rhythm of life as we experience it: decline, fall, rise, renovation. Jesus himself reminds us: 'Unless a wheat grain falls on the ground and dies, it remains only a single grain; but if it dies, it yields a rich harvest' (John 12:24). This is the rhythm of the seasons; it is the sequence of the day; it is the same rhythm that belongs to the whole process of human existence. When a child is born it is separated from the life of total protection and experiences a sense of being alone and exposed. This is the child's first experience of dying. Yet dying is the price of being born, both in infancy and in adult life. Memories of wedding bliss may speedily recede as, financially, things get tough and the care of small children makes increasing psychological and emotional demands. The love that is called for in the experience of marriage and in the experience of being a parent is love unto death and loving someone in the midst of all weaknesses and failings. In many ways, therefore, the experience of life itself prepares us for death.

Support of the Community

We are helped, too, to face up to our own death by experiencing the reaction of the community to the deaths of others. A community that is not afraid to gather round its dying and to be fully present to the bereaved, helping them to rebuild their lives, is by that very fact building up the faith and hope of the community and providing almost a tangible presence of the caring and compassionate God. Bereavement is the price we pay for loving and there is nothing we can say that will take away the pain. Neither should children be shielded from the reality of death and loss but should be gently drawn into the mystery of death and included at funerals. Seeing life in very simple terms they can often give much support, aid and relief to a bereaved person. Out of such experiences within the community, we can be confident that we shall not be alone when our need to belong is most acute.

Communion of Saints

The mourner's real concern is communion with those who have died. It is the presence of the dead that is missed and mourned. That is why for centuries the Church has encouraged faith in the communion of saints, where living and dead communicate life to each other. This is one of the greatest mysteries of our faith impressing upon us that fellowship with our loved ones does not cease with death. Through prayer in Christ we are able to remain forever in communion with those who have gone before us in faith thereby enabling us to resume life with renewed strength and a great sense of healing. In the words of George Maloney:

> 'If you take this ancient doctrine of the communion of saints seriously, you should be able to walk and talk with your departed ones. The love of God in them that still binds them closely to you becomes the powerful wavelength by which they can communicate with you. The greater your love for them, the greater the communication.'[6]

GROUNDS FOR HOPE IN ETERNAL LIFE

Resurrection at the Heart of Life

Just as death belongs to the heart of the whole process of living, so too does resurrection. For wherever there is death, in whatever form it threatens us, there we believe is the promise of eternal life. It does not come to us simply at the moment of terminal death; the resurrection is a present reality disclosing the power of God's grace operating in every moment here and now.

'In the midst of a wounded world, you can still hear the heart-beat of God's creation: without a sign of hope today, parents live for tomorrow; residents make plans for their environment when experience says that all their efforts will be fruitless. It is not the powerlessness, but the resilience and power of such people to stay alive in the midst of social neglect that is most striking.'[7]

This point is repeatedly emphasised by the scriptures, but in a special way by St John: 'Whoever believes in the one who sent me has eternal life . . . such a person has passed from death to life' (John 5:24); And again: 'Eternal life is this: to know you, the only true God, and Jesus Christ whom you have sent' (John 17:3).

Attitude of Jesus During Life

We can only believe in eternal life now because of what has happened in Jesus Christ. He is the guarantee of our continuing hope, of an eventual end to darkness, of the promise that, in spite of present appearances, all will finally be well. Throughout his life, Jesus confirmed the passionate devotion of God to his people – a love which is utterly inexhaustible and extravagant, constantly assuring us of healing, forgiveness and newness of life. He spoke of God, who is our Father – that lover of life who made us out of his love and has destined us to live with him forever. Throughout his life, Jesus was known as the friend of sinners; he sat down at table and ate with them (Mark 2:15-17). Many of his parables speak of God going in search of what has been lost and, in the end, of God's kingdom being promised to 'tax-collectors and harlots'. Jesus went even further: when the human response was struck dumb or, as happened so often during his life, was reduced to mocking laughter, he restored to life the widow's son at Nain and raised Lazarus his friend who had spent four days in the tomb. It is difficult for us to imagine such incredible happenings in the life of Jesus but, in a dramatic way, they speak to us of a life that knows no bounds and considers no situation beyond redemption. All who came into the company of Jesus in faith experienced him as life and resurrection.

The Attitude of Jesus Towards His Own Death

But the greatest testimony of Jesus lies in the way he faced up to his own death. He spoke about it with equanimity: 'I am the good Shepherd, I know my own and my own know me, just as the Father knows me and I know the Father and I lay down my life for my sheep' (John 10:14). And again: 'I tell you this now, before it happens, so that when it does happen you may believe that I am he'. (John 13:15). When the moment of his death arrived, there is no doubt that Jesus experienced the full horror of a painful and excruciating death. St Mark refers to 'sudden fear and great distress'; Luke describes the anguish and the sweat that fell to the ground like great drops of blood; and both Matthew and Mark contain that cry of abandonment uttered by Jesus in the moment of his death. Jesus really entered into the darkness of death, crying out to the one who had the power to save him out of death.

And yet we know that this darkness was not the ultimate fact in the life of Jesus. In him the face of death was changed dramatically; what had once been the symbol of an absurd self-assertion and had set the face of everyone against God (Genesis 3:5) is now inwardly transformed and becomes the symbol of the measure of God's love for us. In John's account, especially, the arrest, trial and crucifixion of Jesus are presented as the triumph of one who freely chose to lay down his life. His final words to the disciples are a kind of commentary on all that was to follow: 'In the world you will have trouble, but be brave; I have conquered the world' (John 16:33). We are told that Jesus, 'knowing everything that was going to happen to him' (John 18:4), carried his own cross and chose the moment of his own death: 'After Jesus had taken the vinegar he said, "It is accomplished"; and bowing his head he gave up his spirit' (John 19:30). Jesus did not die into nothingness. In the light of the resurrection, we know that the Father was there to receive him and because of that we know that Good Friday is always followed by Easter Day, just as surely as Spring follows Winter. We can now hold fast to the testimony of Jesus because he demonstrated in dramatic terms that self-offering love is the only force in the world strong enough to overcome death. From the depths of despair and nothingness, he has given us the pledge of new hope and new life. To know that love here and now is to have eternal life.

ETERNAL LIFE: HEAVEN OR HELL?

Although we have no direct experience of what lies beyond death, by listening more attentively to the testimony of Jesus we can understand something of what lies in store for us. And this means that we must not ignore what he has to say about the possibility of hell.

Hell as an Option

We are familiar with myths of the past: graphic descriptions of damnation and hell-fire such as we find in James Joyce's *Portrait of the Artist as a Young Man*. Such descriptions, however, in more recent times have become such a matter for ridicule that practically all mention of hell has disappeared. It is hardly mentioned at all, for example, in the documents of the Second Vatican Council[8] which sought to overcome people's fear of God and to promote a God of love and mercy. People must not be frightened into goodness by what has been described as 'the great theatre of torments' and 'the howling criminal warehouses of hell'.

Nevertheless, Jesus did use stark images of destruction and consuming suffering. He speaks of the possibility of being cast into outer darkness (Matthew 5:29-30) and bystanders are warned: 'Strive to enter by the narrow door; for many, I tell you, will seek to enter and will not be able' (Matthew 7:13-14). He frequently emphasises the urgency of his message: 'If your right hand should be your downfall, cut it off and throw it away; for it will do less harm to lose one part of yourself than to have your whole body go to hell' (Matthew 5:29-30); and again, he doesn't hesitate to use the image of fire burning: 'And if your eye should be your downfall, tear it out; it is better for you to enter into the kingdom of God with one eye than to have two eyes and be thrown into hell where their worm will never die nor their fire go out' (Mark 9:48).

What are we to make of the use of this imagery by Jesus? First of all, it speaks of the possibility of refusal at the heart of our covenant relationship with God. The salvation which God extends to us is personal love which calls forth nothing less than personal love in return. It represents the helplessness of God who is tied by the logic of his own love which fully respects the gift of freedom he has granted to each of us. His love for us must reckon with the possibility of our refusing that love.

But, secondly, the consequences of our refusing that love lie not only in the future. Whilst hell for all eternity might be impossible for us to imagine, we cannot deny the 'man-made' hells which surround us on earth: there is the widespread violation of human rights with millions of people trapped in dire poverty, many innocent people captured and imprisoned for political dissent, and young children abused and murdered. We cannot deny the fact of our inhumanity and the hellish behaviour it engenders. And so it must come as no surprise that Jesus, with all the urgency that he can muster, wants us to face up to the moral choice that confronts us and to recognise that only the power of his grace can save us now and for all eternity (cf Catechism par. 1033-1037).

Heaven as a Fact

Whilst hell is a possibility, it remains only a possibility. We have no way of knowing whether anyone inhabits hell or not. What we do know, however, is that God's mercy and love go beyond all imagining and so when we speak of heaven, within the context of faith we are speaking of a certainty. In Romans 8, St Paul lists the worldly powers he had experienced: life and death, the world and all its powers, good and evil, things present and things to come, all creation – and then he says that nothing can separate us from the love of God in Christ Jesus our Lord. We must gradually come to the realisation that, in spite of everything, we are somehow mysteriously surrounded by the victory of Jesus Christ, and from that we get our courage. Through Christ we are already beyond time and the power of time, beyond sin and the weight of the flesh, beyond death. Knowing God as he is we already belong to heaven.

One description of the kingdom summarising the teaching of Jesus about the qualities that make for eternal happiness is contained in the beatitudes of the Sermon on the Mount. In the kingdom of heaven, Jesus tells us, we are healed of sorrow and comforted, when 'God will wipe away every tear from our eyes' (Revelation 21:4). We shall have the earth for our heritage, Jesus continues. We shall possess the good qualities of the earth as our very own; all that we truly value on earth and much beyond our wildest imaginings will be there for us to enjoy to the full in the kingdom. The positive human developments of this world are a foretaste of that which the eye has not seen nor ear heard that God has prepared for those who love him. We shall finally be satisfied; those who have experienced hunger and thirst will no longer suffer deprivation and poverty. We will experience love beyond measure and become the people we have always wanted to be. Jesus compares such satisfaction to a treasure hidden in a field (Matthew 13:44), and to a pearl of great price (Matthew 13:45).

Most of all, Jesus assures us, we shall experience forgiveness, mercy and love. We have already mentioned the fears of judgement that have darkened the lives of many Catholics within the Church. Faith in the kingdom means believing that Jesus will deliver us from the wrath to come. As risen Lord, his first words to the disciples were words of peace and forgiveness; throughout his life, he was completely at one with his message: 'I came not to call the righteous, but sinners' (Mark 2:17). It is this same Jesus, the preacher of God's forgiveness, who is our judge. It is inconceivable that we could be judged on any other criterion than that love, or that the judge himself, could ever be other than merciful and compassionate. We shall then know what it is to be loved by God. (cf Catechism par. 1021-1022: 'At the evening of life, we shall be judged on our love'. John of the Cross).

Such an experience of mercy and forgiveness means that the kingdom of heaven is essentially a fellowship when we shall join the great company of saints. In particular, we shall be united with all those whom we have known and loved on earth: our mothers and fathers, brothers and sisters, and our many relatives and friends to whom we are personally indebted for our faith in Jesus, a reunion without fear or threat of further separation. With them, we shall see face to face the God who is the source of all good, that lover of life whose imperishable spirit is in all. In the Scriptures, God's love for his people is frequently compared to the bond of marriage. The ecstatic experience of a husband and wife who are deeply in love is regarded as the only adequate language in which to express the warmth and affection of God's love. Such an experience, Jesus tells us, is only a pale shadow of that love which awaits us in the kingdom where we shall be truly surprised by joy. 'In death we meet the conqueror of death; me meet love' (cf Catechism par. 1023-1029).

NOTES

1 St Therese of Lisieux, *Her Last Conversations* (Washington 1977), p. 30
2 cf Eamon Duffy, *The Stripping of the Altars* (Yale 1992), pp. 300ff
3 A Solzhenitsyn, *Cancer Ward* (Penguin 1970), pp. 110-111
4 cf Nicholas Lash, *Death and Resurrection* in *Catholic Medical Quarterly* (July 1973), p. 107
5 cf Nicholas Lash, art. cit., p. 109
6 George Maloney, *Everlasting Now* pp. 98-99 (cf Catechism pars. 957-959 and par. 1032)
7 Austin Smith, *Passion for the Inner City* (Sheed & Ward 1985), p. 68
8 cf Vatican II, *Lumen Gentium*, no. 48

FURTHER READING

Catechism of the Catholic Church: pars. 998-1050
Harvey, Peter, *Death's Gift* (Epworth Press 1985)
Hellwig, Monika, *What are they saying about Death and Christian Hope?* (Paulist Press, 1978)
Lash, Nicholas, *Death and Resurrection* (Catholic Medical Quarterly 1973)
Maloney, George, *The Everlasting Now* (Ave Maria 1980)

ACKNOWLEDGEMENTS

I would like to thank the people of St Clare's in Liverpool for their constant inspiration and support in faith; the Rev. Aelred Smith for his many scriptural insights and for providing the Foreword; and Sister Alice Simm for her encouragement in helping me to persevere with the task.

All scriptural texts are taken from the New Jerusalem Bible, published and copyright 1985 by Darton, Longman and Todd Ltd and DoubleDay & Co Inc. and are used by permission of the publishers.